If Y...
THI...
You
CAN!
for
TEENS

Other books, audio, and training programs by TJ Hoisington

Return to Robinson Island

If You Think You Can!

Maximizing Human Performance

Maximizing Sales Performance

Maximizing the Customer Service Experience

The Power of Unconventional Leadership

The Power to Shape Your Life

Inspirational Thoughts, Insights, and Truths

Achieving Success in Sales

If You THINK *You* CAN!

for TEENS

Thirteen Laws for
Creating the Life of Your Dreams

TJ HOISINGTON

AYLESBURY
PUBLISHING

ISBN 0-9758884-9-8

Printed in the United States of America.

Paperback Edition
10 9 8 7 6 5 4 3 2 1

To my wonderful children –
Bryce, Connor, Kyla, and Julia.
I wish you much success and happiness
throughout your lives!
You give me great joy!

"We are all living in cages with the doors wide open."
— George Lucas, the creator of **Star Wars**

CONTENTS

PREFACE

. . . .

I HAVE ALWAYS BEEN FASCINATED BY achievement. Starting at a young age, this fascination has led me to study its laws and principles in depth. In fact, half of my life has been devoted to better understanding this phenomenon.

Today, as I travel the country speaking to audiences of all kinds, I have come to realize that many students and teenagers are ill equipped to achieve in life. Just as there are certain laws that govern nature, like gravity, mass and momentum, and $E=mc^2$, there are also laws that govern performance and achievement. Unfortunately, either people are unaware of them, and therefore don't align themselves accordingly, or they simply do not apply them. Far too many enter into adulthood ill equipped to succeed. As a result, many people chase after goals and find that the results they desire constantly elude them. But you have a choice!

For this reason, I have written this book geared toward teens. It is filled with rich and moving stories of both successes and failures. It is also filled with true principles and insights that, when applied, will help you achieve whatever you want in life.

As part of my research, I went back to some of the classic books and greatest writings of all time. I studied the greatest achievers and discovered what made them great and what helped them to obtain their desired results. Then I made those distinctions easy for all people to understand and embrace. I have also used some of my own successes and failures to illustrate the applicability of these ageless principles. But remember, the power is in the principles—not the stories!

In my research and in life I have found that there are thirteen fundamental laws or principles that govern achievement. We live in a time where self–help and finding fulfillment seems to dominate the bookshelves, yet I have specifically written about the art of achievement. If there is something you want to achieve, this is the book for you.

The purpose of this book is to remind you what *is* possible and *how* it is possible. As you read this short and concise book, you will have frequent and powerful "aha" moments. There is an old saying, "When the student is ready, the teacher will appear." These pages are filled with powerful stories and examples that will move and inspire you to take action and make these time–tested principles work in your life.

Note: To get the most out of this book, I recommend that you read with a pen. Underline and make notes in the margins based on impressions that come to you. This will help you understand and retain these powerful principles more effectively.

CHAPTER 1

THE GREATNESS WITHIN YOU

ONCE UPON A TIME THERE WERE DREAMS—*dreams of greatness*. A time when people started out wanting to be somebody. A time when they wanted to achieve something, to get somewhere. You can probably relate to lying on your bed or sitting in class dreaming of what you want for your life. Unfortunately, along the way, millions have forgotten that we are the masters of our own fate and creators of our own destiny. As time passes, many have given up on the idea that big dreams and goals are achievable. Far too many graduate from school and step into the real world only to lose sight of all the possibilities that surround them.

In 1957, members of a Thailand monastery were put in charge of moving a large clay statue of Buddha to a new location. As the crane lifted the statue, the weight was so great that the statue began to crack. Worse yet, it started to rain. In fear of seriously damaging the statue, they lowered it, placed a tarp over it, and decided to continue the following morning. That night, while one of the monks was inspecting the statue with a flashlight, he noticed a reflection shining from out of a crack that was forming in the clay. Out of curiosity he retrieved a hammer and chisel, and started chipping away. Finally, after much of the clay had been removed, he realized that it was not a clay statue at all, but rather a large, solid-gold Buddha.

Many historians believe that several hundred years earlier, the Thai monks had covered the golden Buddha with clay in an effort to disguise it from the Burmese army. A battle ensued and consequently the Thai monks were destroyed, and it wasn't until 1957 that the true nature of the Buddha was discovered. Today, the golden Buddha rests in a temple in Thailand, open to the public.

Like the Buddha, we all have great potential and untold wealth within. Yet, due to the battles of life, we too can find it difficult to see beyond our own layers of clay.

"Champions are born and then unmade."
—Converse

Some years ago Converse, the athletic shoe company, promoted this ad: "Champions are born and then unmade."

The ad implied that the innate greatness we possessed the moment we came out of the womb would soon be replaced with limitations and defeat. We were born to win, yet soon we are conditioned and programmed to lose.

Starting in childhood, conditioning is a gradual, yet consistent and relentless progression. Did you know that the average fourth-grade child has heard the words, "No, you can't do that" over seventy thousand times? Unfortunately, for many this is just the beginning of the destructive conditioning that will be pounded into their heads for years to come. Maybe you have already experienced this conditioning in your life. For example, if you were asked a question in class and gave the wrong answer maybe that day you decided, "I'm never going to raise my hand again."

I can certainly remember in grade school the teacher asking for a volunteer to spell the word "they". I knew I could spell it. I was sure I could. So, I raised my hand high and confidently. Waving my hand to get my teacher's attention, she called on me and I spelled it, "t-h-A-y". Waiting for my teacher to say, "you are correct!" She instead said, "You are WRONG!" Now that might not seem like a real big thing to you, but for me it was shattering. Not only was it the words she used, but also it was the way she said, "you are wrong!" that caused the rest of the class to laugh at me. I was embarrassed. I wanted to climb into a corner somewhere and hide. From that time forward, coupled with other similar situations, I chose not to speak in class. I quickly learned it was easier and safer not to say anything at all. Buck Minister Fuller put it this way, "All children are born geniuses; 9,999 out of every 10,000 are swiftly, inadvertently *de*geniusized by grown-ups."

Even as we get older we make settlements—settling for less than our true potential—as a result of what someone said or did. Maybe we had a goal, and out of our excitement we shared the goal with someone we admired only to hear them say, "You are going to do what?" "You can't do that." "You've never done something like that before." "You don't have the education, money, talent, etc." Besides, "You are too young." They questioned our abilities, and in that vulnerable moment, we believed them. Therefore, you must be careful what you allow into your mind and except as reality.

In his book *Love and Awakening*, John Welwood uses the analogy of a castle to illustrate this conditioning process. If you are not aware or prepared, this scenario I am about to explain could happen to you. Imagine yourself being a magnificent castle with thousands of rooms. Each room is elegant, even perfect. You love each room for its uniqueness, how magnificent it is, and for its character. Then imagine one day someone coming into one of your rooms and boldly telling you that the room was ugly, worthless, or unacceptable. Consequently, out of your need to be loved and accepted, you found yourself closing the room off from the rest of the world. Then imagine if most everyone else who entered your castle over a period of time also thought that many of your rooms were imperfect and needed to be changed to their liking. One after another, slowly and systematically, imagine each door being closed. Eventually, you realize that by closing off these parts of you—your castle, or your dreams, that it actually started making you feel safe. Soon you found yourself living in a castle with a thousand rooms—occupying only one or two. In this book are the tools that will prevent this from happening to you. If applied, the next few pages will put you in the driver's seat toward success.

Far too many of us are guided by the limiting belief that high achievers simply have superior talents and that is why they are successful. It is the, "you just have it or you don't" mentality. Well, research indicates that in most cases the opposite is true. After a five-year study of 120 top artists, athletes, and scholars, Dr. Benjamin Bloom

> "The easier it is to be GOOD, the harder it is to be GREAT!"

and his research team determined that success was more about "drive and determination, not great natural talent." In fact, the belief that they were special surfaced long before any signs of greatness or talent were noticed. Dr. Bloom went on to say that even the mothers of those studied said, "It was their other child [brother or sister] who had the greater gift." As the saying goes, "Sometimes those who are given more end up with less, and those who are given less end up with more." Maybe you have noticed at times that the more talent someone has, the lazier they are. I'm going to show you throughout this book that regardless of whether or not you possess talent or any other special advantage, your dreams are possible.

This was the case with Will Kellogg, who was reported to be a shy man with few friends, limited interests, and no discernible talents. Will was forty-six years of age before he made the decision to go into business for himself. (You don't have to wait until you are forty-six to succeed.) At the time he was working for his older brother, Dr. Kellogg, who never paid Will more than $87 in a month.

One day, while Will and Dr. Kellogg were experimenting to improve the food for his patients, they discovered "flakes" by accident. Will had left a pot of boiling wheat to stand a little too long. When the wheat became tempered, he rolled it into a flake. Will tried convincing his brother to mass-market the discovery, but Dr. Kellogg refused. He doubted Will's idea. As a result, in 1906 Will decided to market the idea on his own and he became one of the richest men in America.

Many are tempted to set their dreams or goals aside before they make the slightest effort to achieve them because of fear. What do they fear? They fear the unknown, failure, what others will think, and they even fear success. As a result, many find themselves living what Henry David Thoreau describes as "lives of quiet desperation." Others unconsciously allow past failures to determine their future. They unceasingly re-live their past attempts and failures. They think because it didn't work out then, it probably won't work out now. They might also worry about what could go wrong in the future and therefore do nothing at all.

It is easy to find reasons why things won't work. The entire world is full of rationales as to why you can't be great. Achievers, however, find the reasons why things will work. For centuries people commonly believed that the earth was at the center of the universe and that the sun revolved around it. Although many great minds disputed this belief, it wasn't until Galileo came along and proved otherwise. In order to do so, he took the leaders of that time to the tower of San Marco, and with his newly perfected telescope, he showed them his discovery. It threatened the leaders of that day because it contradicted their strongly held beliefs. The leaders became angry and even tortured Galileo in an effort to get him to retract his position. Eventually he did just that in February, 1633. Out of fear for his life, he retracted his beliefs.

Like the leaders during the time of Galileo, people who can't see new possibilities for themselves are unlikely to see new possibilities for you. People are certain they know what's best for you and often conclude you don't have what it takes. Your friends—even your closest teachers, parents, and family members may try their hardest to prevent you from taking the leap. They may talk you out of going for your dreams. If you are not careful, you too could be pressured into retracting your own beliefs and dreams.

There's a crucial time when you need to tune out the critics and a time when you must cease from seeking their approval. Cavett Robert said that there are many people who don't want to take the trip themselves, yet pose as experts who criticize the travels of others. These are not the people with whom you want to associate—they are toxic.

> There's a crucial time when you need to tune out the critics...

It's a choice not to turn your happiness over to other people, or let others control you. You wouldn't turn your circulatory system over to other people. You wouldn't turn your respiratory system over to other people. But you will let someone say a snide remark and it will cause you to crawl around campus for two days saying, "Where did I go wrong? I'm not good enough" or "Nobody likes me."

You must also stop worrying what others think of your clothes, weight, the pimple face or the car you may drive. Gosh, do you really think any of these things matter long-term anyway? I like Dr. Daniel Amen's 18/40/60 rule: *When you are 18, you worry about what others are thinking of you; when you are 40 you don't give a darn what others think of you; when you are 60 you realize that nobody has been thinking of you at all.* Did you get that? People aren't sitting around thinking about you. Most people spend their time thinking about themselves; their own problems, challenges, and opportunities. By the way, what do you think everyone's favorite subject is? It's themselves! For example, when you show up at school worrying about being accepted or how you look that day, what do you think everyone else is thinking about? It's *themselves!* Maybe, your friends are worrying about doing well on a test or being noticed. Regardless of what others are thinking the subject is always the same—*themselves!*

So, begin today by investing your time thinking about your dreams and future that desperately awaits your arrival—and begin finding ways to effectively make them a reality! Remember that you are ultimately in competition with no one but yourself—the very best you that you are capable of being.

The truth is, you are powerful beyond measure, even though there is a part of you that would have you believe otherwise. When the pressure is on, there lies in all of us the temptation to compromise for being average and to live a life of mediocrity—to take the path of least resistance and go along with the crowd. This is easy to do. We may ask ourselves whether or not we really do have what it takes to achieve our dreams. In their book, *I Want to Change, but I Don't Know How*, Tom Rusk and Randy Read eloquently relate that people frequently go through life playing it safe. Why? Because it gives them the permission to believe, "If I never let myself feel too good, maybe I'll never get hurt too badly."

Gandhi, Grandma Moses, Steven Spielberg, Rosa Parks, Steve Jobs, and Oprah Winfrey; each of these individuals stand as examples of what is possible. They have managed to break the rules, stretch the limits, and even make history. Many began their efforts toward success at your age. So this begs the questions: If they can do it ...why not you? What about your greatness? You have it, but have you tapped into it? If so, how much? How can you draw on more of your greatness and begin living your dreams and achieving your goals?

Although inspired by greatness, we sometimes doubt our own potential. Maybe we know that something is possible, but we just aren't confident that it is possible for ourselves, given our current abilities or our past. We think, "I don't have any special talents." "I don't have what they have." "I could never do that." Stop! You must come to grips with the fact that within you exists the same powerful abilities that enables winners to be winners—you simply must choose to apply them. There comes a time when you must re-enter your castle rooms that you have closed off from the rest of the world and pull up the blinds and open the windows, allowing fresh air and light to enter. Decide you are going to defy the odds. Decide that you are going to stop allowing others to limit you. Decide that you are going to make it happen—starting now. Today is your chance to begin designing the life of your dreams. The fact that you are young and are being exposed to these principles is the best time to make this decision and can make all the difference in your future.

Extraordinary people are simply ordinary people that do extra ordinary things. Many of them did not have the education, talent, resources or other special advantages. Many were young. All of them had fears and insecurities. Oprah Winfrey came from a dysfunctional and abusive childhood. Einstein didn't speak until he was four years old. His teacher described him as "mentally slow, unsociable, and adrift forever in his foolish dreams." Others were in debt to the hilt. Thomas Edison only had three months of formal education. William Lear, the creator of Lear Jet Corporation, dropped out of school in the sixth grade. Yet, each of these achievers and many more have gone on to become great successes. In fact, did you know that 20% of America's millionaires never set foot in college? Did you know that 21 of the 222 Americans listed as billionaires in 2003 never got their college diplomas and two of them never finished high school? So although

> Most Important:
> You **must**
> BELIEVE IN
> YOURSELF.

learning and personal growth is essential for success, a formal degree is important and beneficial, but it does not guarantee success. *The most important ingredient that determines whether or not you succeed is the power of believing in yourself.* This is the common thread that is unquestionably weaved among all achievers. Nothing is more important than first having a belief in yourself.

Ultimately, it is not the external circumstances or conditions that limit you. It is you! It is your negative thoughts, comfort zones, self-defeating habits, poor strategies, blame lists, or even your failure to continuously educate yourself and grow. You are the greatest obstacle in life that prevents you from going from where you are, to where you want to be. The earlier you realize and decide that you are the single most determining factor as to whether or not you succeed or fail, only then will your life have a chance to improve.

The wonderful part of all this is that you can change. You can grow. You can rise above your challenges and start producing the results you desire. People like yourself do it all the time. No matter how difficult your circumstances may seem at this moment, possibilities are always available to you. Carl Joseph was born with one leg. As a teenager he decided to play football in high school without using crutches or an artificial leg. He worked so hard that eventually he made All-State defensive lineman. The local newspapers said, "He ran so smoothly and so effortlessly that when you watched him run you could hardly tell he was missing a leg. Especially when he was chasing down the quarterback from behind." In basketball he did slam dunks, and in track he could jump five feet ten inches—all with one leg. In fact, even with his disadvantage, he went on to receive a four-year athletic training scholarship from the University of Pittsburgh. He said, "It is all in the mind. My mind always told me that I could do things, and I just went and did them. I never worried that I couldn't do something, I just did it. You just keep trying, and you will always get there." Despite an apparent limitation, what enabled Carl to go for it? What secret did he possess when others would have given up? What specific habits did he form that made dunking a basketball or receiving a full-ride scholarship possible? Continue reading—the answers will be shared throughout this book!

What about those who convince themselves that they are too young and inexperienced to have success? I too found myself giving in to this way of thinking and it has accounted for numerous opportunities on which I neglected to act. I also notice others, who were once convincing themselves that they were too young to achieve a particular goal and now they are convincing themselves they are too old. The fact is, neither is true! Age is not a prerequisite for success.

For instance, actors Matt Damon and Ben Affleck were eleven years old when they found a quiet area in the school cafeteria and held meetings to talk about their latest acting projects. At fifteen years old, George Parker created one of the most successful games ever produced—*Monopoly*. What was the secret that led two young men to create the Internet search engine, *Google* or three young men to create the video sharing website, *YouTube*—and turn them both into billion-dollar successes? The list could go on and on with other examples, such as *Facebook's* founder Mark Zuckerberg and even the legendary co-founder of *Apple Inc.*, Steve Jobs, when he started *Apple* at twenty-one years old. What secret did these individuals possess that enabled them to create enormous success at such a young age?

At the other end of the age spectrum, I constantly find myself reminding adults to dream again—that their dreams are still available to them. Too many adults have gotten comfortable with their situation and given up on their goals—a pattern that likely started as a teenager or young adult. As you'll read later in this book, it is easy to give up.

Yet there are many who decide that it's not over until it's over and they defy the odds. Like Norman MaClean, who was seventy-three years old and rejected the idea of retirement. Having taught literature at the University of Chicago for thirty years, he still felt something tugging at him. He wondered if he too could be a writer, so he went to his cabin in Montana and spent the next two years writing. At the end of this time, his writings were published in a book called *A River Runs Through It*, which eventually became a movie.

When it comes to age, George Eliot said, "It is never too late to be what you might have been." Anna Mary Robertson Moses began sketching at a very young age. Intrigued by every little detail, she began using berries to bring more color into her paintings. As life would have it, she was forced to put her paintings on hold because of the demand of her family's farm. For sixty years she didn't paint at all. Finally, in 1938 she retired from farming and once again took up painting. By the time of her death, twenty-three years later, she had painted thousands of scenes remembered from her

> Your past does not *have* to equal your future.

childhood and became known around the world as Grandma Moses. What was the unique formula that led Grandma Moses to leave such a lasting legacy? What was the secret of Norman MaClean? Is there something they understood that others didn't?

I don't know your age or what your current circumstances look like. I don't know what your past was like, and I definitely don't know what the future holds for you. You are the only person who can make that determination. This, however, is what I do know: Your past does not have to equal your future. You can decide today to begin designing a great life for yourself and your future family by simply putting into action the principles in this book.

J.K. Rowling understood the principles outlined in this book, even if she wasn't consciously aware of them. She dealt with poverty, unemployment, and being a single mother, yet stayed true to her personal vision. At one point life was so difficult that she went on welfare, and made only $105 per week. It was reported that in an effort to save every penny, she cut back on meals and spent all day in local cafes in an attempt to save on her heating bill at home. At the cafes she would write on note pads while her daughter Jessica napped beside her.

Although Rowling experienced severe episodes of depression, she was determined to complete her book and have it accepted. After waiting three years for a response, she finally published her book and the Harry Potter phenomenon began. Since then, over 250 million of her books have been sold worldwide and Rowling was named the world's best-paid author of all time—with her worth reaching over one billion dollars. J.K. Rowling knew what it would take to turn her dream into reality. Do you?

Oliver Wendell Holmes said, "What lies behind us and what lies before us are tiny matters compared to what lies within us." I'm presuming that you are reading this book because you believe in what's possible or you have the desire to believe in possibilities. Maybe you want to get somewhere and achieve something great. Maybe you're searching for that one idea or distinction that will give you the slight edge. It's likely you want a book that will be a source of inspiration for you or a friend. If any of the above are true, then you are reading the right book.

> "All achievement is the choice of thoughts and activities."

Like the *laws of nature*, there are laws that govern your performance, and thereby your achievement. You can either ignore these laws or you can effectively apply them to get whatever you want from life.

If you are reading this book, yet content with where you are and desire for no more than what you already have, then this book will simply serve as a enjoyable read. Hopefully, you want more—even if it is a little more than what you currently have. Whether it's the desire for a better relationship, a great job, financial success, or spirituality—the principles in this book will help you achieve these goals.

I'm reminded of my first teacher who said, "Achievement is a choice of thoughts and activities." Today is your time to step up. Believe in yourself. Defy the odds. Stop seeking the approval of others and begin putting a plan in place to start consciously taking charge of your future.

In the following pages you will learn about *thirteen laws* that govern the achievement of any goal. My advice as you read this book is to first believe in the amazing reality that dreams are possible. Goals, whether large or small, are achievable. I promise that *if you think you can...you can.*

Second, apply the time-tested laws and complete the exercises at the end of each chapter. It's your choice to not only read them, but to also apply them. Boldly and confidently put them to work, and you will experience their true merit.

CHAPTER 2

THE POWER OF DECISIONS

Law #1

JUST AS GREAT POWER EXISTS WITHIN a tiny seed, explosive power resides within you and your decisions are the means to unleashing that power. In order to turn a life dream into reality, you must begin with a decision. I have chosen this law to be the first because decisions literally shape your destiny at every level. Every other law or principle discussed in this book are subject to the fact that you have a choice. So let's get started.

Unlike animals, you do not have to fall victim to a genetic code or the conditioning of your past. You don't have to allow life's circumstances to determine your destiny. If you consider yourself stuck, you don't have to remain stuck. If you are unhappy and feel you are moving in the wrong direction, you can decide to change. Decisions are the force that changes your direction in a moment's notice.

Every person on the planet possesses a power called "free agency," which is the power to make decisions. We all have the freedom to decide what we want to think. We all have the power to choose our behaviors and therefore our outcomes. Some have used this freedom to choose noble endeavors while others have chosen otherwise. I'm sure you know people like this. Whether good or bad, all achievement is the direct result of thoughts and decisions. Let's take a look at the enormous power that decisions can play in our lives.

It was in a moment of decision that Rosa Parks had a great impact on the Civil Rights movement. In 1955 she refused to give up her seat on a crowded bus to a white man—a decision that changed a nation. That single decision led to a series of events that moved America closer to racial equality. It reflected the explosive effect that one decision can have.

It was also a series of poor decisions that led to the deaths of Elvis Presley, John Belushi, Kurt Cobain, and many others. Even when you look at the radical differences between Gandhi and Hitler, it was not only their ideals, but also their decisions that led to their actions that determined their place in history.

One year in high school a group of friends decided

to go skiing for the weekend. The night they were returning home they began goofing off as they were driving down the road. The car they were driving was the type where the key could be removed from the ignition and the car would continue running, which was exactly what one of the friends did. Driving down the road, one of the friends quickly pulled the key out of the ignition and threw it out the window. They thought it was funny and everyone began laughing. Then they quickly stopped the car and began searching the road for the key. The area where the key had been tossed out was in the middle of a sharp corner. Unfortunately, as the driver was searching for the key, a car came speeding around the corner running into my friend and killing him instantly.

As you can see, we don't always recognize the impact of our decisions. For most of our decisions, the effect doesn't reveal itself until months or even years down the road. Other times we make decisions that have instantaneous consequences. Just remember: we all make decisions that at times seem inconsequential, yet have far-reaching outcomes.

> "Just remember: we all make decisions that at times seem inconsequential, yet have far-reaching outcomes."

Think for a moment about the decisions you made this morning. When you awoke, did you quickly get out of bed or did you lie there debating, in an effort to gain a few more minutes of sleep? What did you eat? Did you leave for school on a positive note, or did you argue with your parents or other family members on your way out the door? When you entered school, what was the first thing you did? Did you greet people with a smile? You probably didn't give those decisions much thought when you made them. However, could they potentially affect your future? Definitely! Imagine for a moment that you slept an extra thirty minutes a day. Could that eventually have a negative impact on a goal that you are working on? You bet! If you ate an unhealthy breakfast or overate, could that have an impact? Sure it could—if you made a consistent habit of it. If you made the decision in your relationships to show more love and patience, could that affect the quality of your relationships? Of course! What about developing good studying habits? The habits you form now will determine the blueprint for which you direct your life.

Again, every decision you make will either keep you on the course to achievement or lead you away from it. It starts with one poor decision that can lead to a series of poor decisions. Rarely does a person lose a relationship overnight. You don't simply wake up one morning having lost weight, nor do you reach the point of obesity immediately after eating. You don't become a chain smoker by smoking one cigarette. What about the friends you hang with? Do you think that the way you dress plays a role in the people you have attracted into your life? Or how people treat you? Again, of course! Neither do you wake up one day with all your goals achieved and living the life of your dreams.

Although these decisions may seem minor and insignificant, they illustrate the point. *Now here is where decisions really shape your destiny*: When you decide to press forward despite defeat. When you decide to take action despite your fears and worries. When you decide to maintain an empowering perspective, even when things aren't going your way. When you decide to grow a backbone and cease to be indecisive! When you make a decision to show more respect for yourself, family, teachers and friends. How about making the decision to stop hanging around with friends that bring you down and have a negative influence on you? These are the decisions that have an explosive impact on your life.

Start right now by making a decision to stop defending your habits. Stop complaining about your circumstances and start doing something about them. Stop blaming others or your past for why you aren't achieving what you want to achieve. Stop being the victim and start saying "no," if necessary. When you are feeling pressured to do things you know you shouldn't be doing, make the decision to say "no". You can also make the decision to be happy from here on out. Make a decision to have higher self-esteem! Make a decision that you are a person worthy of your goals! Most importantly, make a decision to believe in yourself!

I repeat, wherever you are today is simply the result of your thoughts and beliefs. These transform into desires, which

> Start right now by making a decision to stop defending your habits.

lead to *decisions*. If you want to change your life, then change your decisions. It's that simple.

Ultimately the type of decisions that will drastically improve your chances of success will be "true decisions." When a true decision is made, you cut yourself off from all other options except those to which you are committed. In his book, *Think and Grow Rich*, Napoleon Hill shared a story of a general who sailed across the sea to engage in a war with another country. He knew that his men would be greatly outnumbered, and that they would need to be highly committed and motivated if they were going to win. Once his army had exited the ship with all their supplies and made it to shore, he ordered the ships to be burned. As his men watched the ships go up in flames, the general turned to them and said, "We either win or die."

The general made a true decision. In fact, the word decision comes from the Latin root meaning "to cut off from." And there comes a time in every person's life when making a true decision is necessary. A decision where you believe so deeply in what you want that there is no option for turning back. For you it might mean making an absolute commitment to study harder, get better grades or be a leader rather than a follower. You could also decide to improve your language or stop drinking.

Getting to the point of making a true decision can take time. Have you ever felt frustrated because you waffle on a decision? I must have tried losing weight a dozen times before I actually did it. I was once forty pounds overweight, but it wasn't until I made a definite decision that I wanted the fat gone that I lost the weight. I had to get to the point where changing my eating and exercising habits lasted more than a few days before falling back into the same old patterns. To become committed, I had to get to the point of do or die. As a result of making this true decision, I naturally and consistently began taking action that led to losing the weight in less than ninety days.

In life, once you make decisions, you must take responsibility for them. On several occasions, I have encountered people who have made poor decisions which caused challenges to enter into their lives. Often these people get discouraged and assume a victim mentality. That leads them to blame life rather than their own decisions that contributed to the problem. They forget, like my friends who were driving back from the skiing trip, that although they have the power to choose, they never have the power to completely choose the consequences of their choices. If you want different outcomes, make new decisions.

One of the great thieves that rob people from making true decisions is *indecision*. What causes indecision? Fear! Fear of making the wrong decision. Fear of what others will think. Fear of the unknown. Fear is the greatest of all thieves. Indecision often has a higher price to be paid than making the wrong decision. Why? Because the price is paid over the long haul in missed opportunities—the very opportunities that can help you achieve what you want.

Any decision is better than no decision. Achievers understand that they will not always make perfect decisions, but they know they can grow from the wrong ones. President Theodore Roosevelt said, "He who makes no mistakes makes no progress." Achievers see each decision and its outcome as stepping-stones toward reaching their final goal.

"He who makes no mistakes makes no progress."

I once had the privilege of speaking to the bestselling author, Charles "Tremendous" Jones. It was at a time in my life when I found myself struggling between staying at or leaving a successful business I had created. My desire was to live my dream, something that required a change in my direction. Although I wanted my dream, I experienced fear. "What if I make the wrong decision?" "What if I don't have what it takes?" I explained my struggle to Mr. Jones, at which point he responded, *"TJ, you weren't born to make right or wrong decisions, you were born to make decisions, and then make them right."*

He wasn't suggesting that you shouldn't strive to make wise decisions. There are times when calculated decisions are necessary. He also wasn't suggesting that there weren't right or wrong decisions in life, because there are. What he meant was even though we know what is best for us, we become paralyzed by fear.

Making decisions requires faith and belief in others and in one's self. It requires faith, which enables us to firmly believe that in the end, things will work out—even if the initial outcome is slightly off course. Often, when we are unable to see the end result or unable to predict the future, we feel the safest decision is to make no decision at all.

In his book, *The Adventure of Leadership*, Hap Klopp the founder of the North Face Company, shares the experience of an expedition that turned disastrous. He told of the Whittaker brothers, Lou and Jim, who lead the expedition. They were tall and strong men standing over six feet. While crossing a glacier in Alaska, one of the members of the expedition team fell and broke his leg. He needed medical attention immediately. They were out in the middle of nowhere on top of Mt. McKinley, and time was running out. As the sun was beginning to go down and the temperature was dropping fast, they radioed for a jet helicopter, but it was unavailable. In its place, a standard helicopter was called to perform the rescue, but it did not do well in high altitudes.

Finally, the helicopter arrived. They quickly loaded the climber into the helicopter, but the added weight of the injured man prevented the helicopter from lifting off the ground. The air was too thin at such a high altitude. As it began getting dark, the Whittakers were forced to improvise.

Hap writes, "They each grabbed a rail of the helicopter and heaved it off the edge of the cliff." The Whittakers watched as the helicopter went down "like a rock through the thin air." Hap adds, "Finally, halfway down, the blades of the helicopter caught air and it flew off toward the hospital." Talk about decisions—that was a big one!

Sometime later, after the experience, Hap asks Jim Whittaker, "What if it didn't work?" Jim replied, "Sometimes you just know." Hap goes on to say, "Obstacles will inevitably pop up on the path to fulfilling your passion, and when they do, like the Whittakers, you must listen to your instinct, your intuition, that little voice deep inside that just knows."

> "Sometimes you just KNOW."

So it is with you. You have that same instinct and intuition. That little voice deep inside you that *just knows*. So be bold, have faith, and make a decision. Make one today ...make one now! And when you are unsure, make the best decision according to your current level of awareness and the resources you have in that moment. Regardless of the outcome, you will have greater knowledge and will be better prepared for what is to come.

When making decisions, keep in mind that as long as the sum total of your good decisions outweighs your poor decisions—you are moving in the right direction.

Starting today I make the true decision to: _____

_____

_____.

CHAPTER 3

DEMANDING THE **BEST** FROM YOURSELF

Law #2

EVERYTHING YOU HAVE RIGHT NOW in your life or will have in your future is a reflection of what you expect to have, and your commitment to it. Aristotle said, "What you expect, that you shall find." In order to get what you want, you must begin expecting and demanding more out of yourself than you currently do. Just like building a muscle, you wouldn't lift the same amount of weight indefinitely and expect muscle to grow. Instead, you would increase the weight, placing greater demand on the muscle. This in turn, would cause the muscle to expand and grow.

A number of years ago, while working with the

bestselling author Anthony Robbins, I learned that there was a big difference between being *interested* in something, and being *committed* to it. Most people are interested in their goals but not truly committed. This prevents them from taking action. In life, we only get what we must have. If you don't *have* to *have* something, it is unlikely you will take the required

Achievers do WHATEVER IT TAKES.

action to achieve your particular goal. When a person is merely interested in a goal, rather than committed to it, they are likely to take action only when it is convenient. On the other hand, people who get what they want make it a habit to do whatever is required—whenever it is required. You can always tell between those who are interested, and those who are committed. How can you tell? Interests and preferences show up in conversation, and commitment shows up in behavior. A committed person goes from thinking, "It would be nice to have this or that" to "I must—I will—I am committed." And then they go and do!

Achievers constantly *demand* more from themselves compared with what the mass majority of people are accepting for themselves. Because they set a high expectation for themselves, they understand that sacrifices will be necessary for a time in order to achieve what they want. When others are relaxing or taking breaks, the achiever continues hustling. John F. Kennedy was referring to achievers when he said they "do what they must—in spite of personal consequences, in spite of obstacles, danger and pressures."

We all have the power to make things happen in our lives. When you want something badly enough you'll do whatever it takes to get it. Even young children have learned this principle. When children truly want something, they become utterly unstoppable. You can tell them "no" a dozen times and they refuse to relent. Finally, they wear you out and you give into their plea.

It will not always be an easy task to achieve a desired result. It is rarely an easy walk in the park. I learned early on that if I truly wanted something, I had to go from doing "just enough" to get by, to really pushing myself. Maybe you can relate. I remember in fourth grade having to be pulled out of social studies class and taken to a special reading class. I was told I was a slow reader and had poor comprehension. I can remember sitting in a very small chair at a very small table reading comic books. After reading, I would take a comprehension test that confirmed what I already suspected—I was not a reader and probably never would be. It was very discouraging.

I remember envying my older brother Steve who read every night before going to sleep. By age eleven he had read all the *Hardy Boys* and *Nancy Drew* books. We shared a bedroom and every night after the lights were turned off, I would ask him to share with me what he read, and he would proceed to tell me. The joy he received from reading was obvious and it inspired me.

Consequently, one day I told my mother I wanted to learn to read like Steve and asked if she would buy me a book. Mother agreed and told me she would do exactly what she did for Steve, which was to buy me my first book and she said once I had read that one, she would buy me another book. Not wanting to copy Steve by reading the *Hardy Boys* or *Nancy Drew* books, I instead chose a different book—the *Bobbsey Twins*. Excitedly, I remember lying down that first night before the lights went off as I started to read. Did I say started to read? That is an overstatement. The moment I started reading the first page I quickly realized how difficult reading was for me. It took real effort. In fact, I can remember struggling through the first page. I read it three or four times, and I still didn't understand what I had read.

That night I was again reminded that, "I must not be a reader—it's not who I am." My whole identity was shaped greatly by this belief. I also thought my brother must have been more talented than I and that a person either has it or they don't. I have since *decided* that this thought is erroneous.

Sometimes we don't change because it is easier to stay the same. In my case I didn't believe in myself and decided to give up. From that day forward, until I reached high school, I hadn't read one book cover to cover. Then one day I was in my father's bedroom when I noticed a cassette tape on his dresser. It was a copied tape that read on one side, *The Day*

My Life Turned Around and on the other side, *How to Live Financially Independent*. At sixteen years old and coming from a large family with little financial means, I was intrigued by these titles.

I put the tape in my pocket and went upstairs to my bedroom that I shared with two other brothers. I put the tape in my Walkman and began listening to concepts and principles for living a successful life. I was amazed by what I was hearing. The tape inspired me so much that I listened to it at least twenty times that first month. The speaker on the tape was my "first" teacher of success principles, Jim Rohn. One of the concepts he taught on that tape was, "If you want your life to change then you must change." He said that you must not wait for your spouse, boss, taxes, or weather to change before you change. Rather, if you will change, your entire world will change. So I had my work cut out for me. He taught that achievers are readers, and I definitely wanted to be an achiever. Like so many at that age, I wanted to be somebody and get somewhere in my life.

That tape led me to many other tapes on the subject, and they all seemed to teach the same message: "all leaders are readers" and that you have to raise your standards and not only expect more, but demand more from yourself. I learned that all you have to do is make it a habit of becoming better than average. Even being slightly better than average can dramatically separate the achievers from the un-achievers. It's the slight edge that makes all the difference.

Finally, the day came when I decided that I didn't want to become a victim of my inability to read. I didn't want that to stand in my way of being successful at whatever I chose. So, I saved up a few dollars and my junior year of high school I purchased my first book, *The Adventure of Leadership* by Hap Klopp. Three or four months later after struggling to read through it, I purchased my second book, *Live Your Dreams* by Les Brown. I read both cover to cover and by the end of my senior year I had read my first two books. It was a major accomplishment for me at that time and today I read a minimum of three to four books per month.

That decision—and my commitment to it—enabled me to turn one of my greatest weaknesses into a useful strength. By taking responsibility for my weakness, I was able to change it, which has greatly shaped who I am today.

I went from saying it *would be nice* to read to *I will* learn to read—no matter what it takes. When you make that type of shift, only then will you hold yourself to a higher standard and begin producing results accordingly. Whatever you decide to go after, you must make an absolute commitment. If you want more out of your job, relationships, health, and life, then you must do whatever is required—and then some.

You must commit yourself to true standards, which are those that you consistently stand by, regardless of their difficulty. These standards are those that you consistently uphold even when no one else is watching. Especially when your parents or teachers are not leaning over your shoulder watching every move. Chris Rock, the comedian is partly known for his dirty mouth, yet at the same time he will not curse in the presence of his mother. I tell my kids to be consistent. Be someone who is honorable whether people are watching or not.

It would have been easier to decide that reading wasn't for me and pursue other goals that didn't require as much effort. However, had I accepted my fate as a non-reader, then in what other areas of my life would I have made compromises? At a young age, I unconsciously knew that if I began settling for less than my true potential, eventually this compromise could become a habit and failure could become my destiny.

It is often easier to lower your standards than it is to raise them. When the pressure is on, it is easier to go along with the masses than it is to separate yourself from them. My advice is that whenever there is doubt between the easier path and the one that requires you to stretch, get in the habit of stretching. Alex Osborne once said, "Unless you are willing to go beyond that which you have already mastered, you will never grow." And growing is the essence of life.

As mentioned earlier, anything you have in your life right now, is a reflection of what you must have. You may want more, but until it becomes a true standard and you

It is often easier to lower your standards than it is to raise them.

demand more from yourself, it will not happen for you. If you want a fulfilling career, attend a prestigious college, have better friends, be popular or whatever the goal may be, then you must commit to step up. As long as your wants remain wishes, it is unlikely you'll ever achieve them. Don't be like the adult who comes home, eats dinner, watches television, and complains about his circumstances, yet does nothing to change them. In other words, good intentions are not enough.

In the future, if you are giving all you have but are miserable at your job and feel you deserve more, then leave. Don't hang around until you're forced out—life is too short. However, if you have decided to continue taking a paycheck, then you owe it to yourself and the company you work for to give your best efforts. The same goes for playing sports or remaining in a relationship. If you have decided these things are really important to you, then get in the habit of giving your best.

I was once told of a builder who had the reputation of being the best builder around. He had worked for years in a large company, and he had reached the age of retirement. Before retiring, his employer asked him to build one more house. The builder accepted this one last job, but his heart was not involved. He used inferior materials and less capable workers. The timber was poor, and he failed to see the many things that should have been clear. When the house was finished, his employer came to him reaching in his pocket and said, "Thank you for all the years you've worked for me. As a gift from me, here is the key. The house is yours. It is a present from me to you." The builder quickly regretted that he had not used the best materials and the most capable workers. If he had only known the house was for him. It doesn't matter whether you choose to be a waiter, lawyer, janitor, nurse, businessperson, but whatever it is, be the best you possibly can.

You and I are the same. The decisions, habits and life we are creating now determine the life we get to live with in the future. In the end, there comes a point when we look back over our lives and determine whether or not we gave it our best. The hope is that you and I can experience what Grandma Moses did when she reached the end of her life and said, "I look back on my life like a good day's work; it is done and I am satisfied with it." If today were your last day to live and you looked over your life, would you be filled with satisfaction and peace, or would you be filled with regret and sadness?

"Life is either a daring adventure or nothing."
–Helen Keller

Helen Keller said, "Life is either a daring adventure or nothing." One way to make it a daring adventure is by raising your standards, make new decisions, even take some risks you know in your gut you need to take.

Holding yourself to higher standards is not always easy. A friend of mine says that there is usually an easier wrong and a harder right. You'll find that when you push yourself, mediocre people won't understand. At times they will think you're crazy and question why you would work so hard? They will ask, why won't you drink? Why won't you have sex or do drugs? But you know deep down that when you do the right thing it brings a sense of fulfillment. Look at all the activities you are engaged in; does it bring out the very best in yourself and others?

One of the best coach's this world has ever seen is Vince Lombardi. Vince wasn't the best or most talented player on his team while growing up, but he was an example of demanding the best from himself. He once played an entire game after getting a cut in his mouth. Following the game, his cut required thirty stitches. Vince refused to give in and willingly endured the pain until the goal was achieved.

This is the level of commitment and demand one must apply to achieve. If it were anything less, more people would be achieving their dreams. *Almost* isn't enough. In the real world, giving it your almost best is not going to cut it. No point intended! It will take, no less than, one hundred percent pure commitment.

Today I make the new commitment to: _____

_____

_____.

CHAPTER 4
· · · · · · · · ·

TAKING THE TIME TO WORK ON YOU

Law #3

I F YOU WANT MORE, THEN YOU MUST become more. In his classic book, *As a Man Thinketh*, James Allen quietly shares a secret that often goes unmentioned. He explains, "Men do not attract that which they *want*, but that which they *are*." Did you catch that?

Whatever you have achieved in your life is a reflection of the person you have *become*. It is a reflection of what you believe is possible, what you truly expect in life, the knowledge you have gained, and habits you have formed. If you want more, then you must become more. It will be necessary that you begin taking the time to improve yourself. Remember:

"The biggest room in the world is the room for improvement."
And no time is better than now!

Just as you cannot give something you don't first have, neither can you achieve something you don't reflect. You may want good grades all day long, but until you apply yourself it's not going to happen. You must instead become, through effort, the type of person who gets good grades. If you want more friends, what type of person must you become in order to have more friends? What must be learned and what skills do you need to develop? For example, it may mean that you must improve your listening skills. Remember: Hearing is a faculty but listening is a skill. When you enter the workforce, remember, the marketplace pays you based on the value that you bring to it. Therefore, what must you do to become more valuable? Otherwise it is simply a wish. This is true with any aspect of your life. You must become the person that will attract what you want.

> "The biggest room in the world is the room for improvement."
> —Unknown

Even if you successfully get what you want, your newfound success may soon disappear if you don't become the person that is equal to or greater than the goal achieved. Think about it. Why is it that new lottery winners lose, squander, or give away their money within a few years of winning it? Why is it that most of them file bankruptcy within five years? The reason is because they have not developed a millionaire mindset. They haven't become the person that is equal to the accomplishment. Therefore, based on the law of attraction, they could not sustain it. Even a mountain climber knows he cannot take short cuts or skip important stages of the climb by simply reaching the summit by helicopter. The climber knows that if he doesn't get properly acclimatized, by ascending gradually, he could become very sick and even die.

Most people are living this principle backward. Instead if living by the philosophy, "Be—Do—Have," they want to "Have—Do—Be." Most people want the interest before they make the investment. They think if they first had a million dollars then they would start doing the things that millionaires do. However, this runs against the laws of nature called the *law of compensation (or law of sowing and reaping)*, which consists of three specific principles. First, is the law of *sowing and reaping*. This means that according to your habits and actions, you attract the results that harmonize with those habits and actions. Therefore, if you are not getting what you want, then change your behaviors.

When you see a champion break a record, it isn't luck. The difference between first place and second place is usually a fraction of a second. What makes the difference? Perhaps the champion practiced a little harder and a little longer than his opponent? Possibly the champion worked on one bad habit long enough so that he was able to replace it with a more empowering habit. Perhaps this was the slight edge that made the difference.

The second part of the law is the law of *increasing returns*. Not only do you reap what you sow, but also you reap more than you sow. If you plant a tiny seed in the ground, you reap a huge tree in return. And the third aspect of the law is *delayed gratification*. This means that you reap what you sow after you have sowed it. If you planted a seed yesterday, it would be foolish to think you could show up today expecting to reap the harvest. The law of the harvest requires patience once you have invested time and energy.

When you see people achieving their goals, you can be sure they have made the commitment to consistently improve upon their skills and abilities. Before a doctor earns one dollar, she has already invested thousands of dollars and time in herself. The same is true with athletes or musicians. They invest countless hours of practice before the opportunity arises to perform. You must do the same. Benjamin Disraeli said, "The secret of success in life is for a man to be ready for his opportunity when it comes." If a person has not prepared himself sufficiently, when the opportunity comes, it is often too late.

I knew that I wanted to be a speaker. I wanted to use my voice as a tool to inspire and give people tools that could improve the quality of their lives. I also realized that if I were to capitalize on potential opportunities that would come my way, I had to develop my skills as a speaker.

While in my early twenties, I worked on the staff of

a senator in Washington, D.C. At midnight, several times a week, I walked a few blocks down the street to the Marriott Hotel, where I proceeded to walk upstairs to the ballroom. Making sure no one saw me, I would walk in, close the door behind me, and proceed to the stage that was set up for the convention the next day. There on the stage, with a big marker in my hand—pretending it was a microphone—I would walk back and forth across the stage speaking to the imagined audience that was sitting before me.

At that time in my life, I was reading every book that had anything to do with public speaking. When I watched a speech by someone who impressed me, I would duplicate his movements and body language. I devoted myself to one skill at a time until it became natural. I practiced my stories over and over to be sure I used the right speed, tone, and expressions until I mastered them. When I didn't go to the hotel, I would listen to audiotapes and read books on performance. When my roommates were watching television, I was in my room studying and planning my future. They would wonder why I worked so hard. They couldn't understand it and would tell me to just relax. They would suggest that I slow down and smell the roses–that should I play today and worry about work tomorrow. Like Garth Brooks says, I would think to myself, "I can smell the roses when I'm running with them in my hands." I kept thinking that if I invested in myself now, the dividends would be paid back in multiple rewards.

If you want to be great at anything, then make the commitment to learn all you can about that subject. Read the books and attend the classes. If you want the results that come from being a better student, athlete, or leader, then commit yourself every day to grow and develop in that area. Listen to the audio programs and read the books. Study those who are achieving what you want to achieve. Bookstores and libraries are filled with answers. When you are driving in your car, turn off the thumping music, for a time, and listen to something that can really make a difference in your life. Earl Nightingale says, "If a person will spend one hour a day on the same subject for five years, that person will be an expert on that subject." When you think about it, that is an amazing promise.

If you have habits that are preventing you from achieving your goals, then rid yourself of them. If procrastination, laziness, overindulgence, or a bad temper is limiting your effectiveness, then go to work to replace those bad habits with good habits.

Improving yourself requires self-discipline. It is not always easy. There will be times when achievement requires you to do things that you don't like to do. Discipline, however, will help you stay on track. It will help you endure to the end without giving into the path of least resistance. Discipline prevents people from engaging in self-indulgent behaviors. People with discipline are in control of themselves and thus have the power to change virtually any aspect of their life.

I suggest that you go from being good to being great in whatever area of personal interest you choose. When you are good, then *good* results are what you will get. And most people are good. Likewise, when you are great, you are more likely to get *great* results. It is a choice! And the only way to become great at any thing is to consistently work at it.

Make the commitment to develop your talents. Most people don't develop talents that come easy to them. Have you ever noticed, the easier it is to be good at something the harder it is to be great? Don't let being good stand in the way of being great! Your talents can be your greatest resource—if you develop them.

> ...the only way to become GREAT is to consistently work at it.

No matter how talented you are, growth is not an automatic process. By default, life creates opportunities by which we grow, such as your girlfriend or boyfriend who decides they don't want to be with you anymore, or experiencing a failing grade, or being cut from the cheerleading squad or football team. However, these growth opportunities will not be enough to take you where you want to go. You must make a deliberate effort to grow and change specifically in alignment with your goals.

Part of the process of improving yourself is learning to take advantage of "feedback." When you begin taking action toward achieving your goals or learning a new skill, you will inevitably start getting feedback. Feedback can be both positive and negative, and both can certainly be very useful, even necessary. For example, positive feedback comes from the feeling of satisfaction, receiving awards, compliments, or simply noticing the results you are producing. As a result of positive feedback, it usually helps people maintain a high level of motivation. Negative feedback, however, may lead some people to question their overall direction. This feedback shows up as pain, disappointment, ridicule, and noticing that you are producing undesirable results.

Feedback, if listened to, is an enormous and necessary asset to achieving your goals. Ignored, it will stifle your chances of achieving your goals. *To achieve your goals more rapidly, decide today to welcome, embrace, and learn from all the feedback you receive.* My one last suggestion with feedback is to take into consideration the source. Lock out the critics. If it is a person, ask yourself, do they have a genuine interest in you achieving your goals? Do they also have the credibility to provide feedback on the matter? If not, then be very selective as to what you accept as useful feedback.

Richard Bandler taught, "The mind likes what is the same, but it learns from what is different." If you neglect to learn from the feedback that comes your way, stay in your comfort zone, or continue in your usual, comfortable patterns, then there is no growth or improvement.

Again, some people don't like changing, because it's easier to stay the same. Some don't change because it leads to uncertainty. Then there are those who don't change, yet expect things to get better around them. What is the definition of insanity? "Doing the same thing and expecting a different result." The only way to grow is to be willing to change.

When you reach a plateau or become stagnant, look within yourself before looking to change what's external. All too often, people rush to change their circumstances instead of changing themselves. Many think that the grass is greener on the other side and rarely is that true. Your success is more likely to happen

What is the definition of INSANITY?

if you will instead ask yourself, "What do I need to do to become better in this area? What skills and habits do I need to form in place of the bad ones, so that I will be led to better circumstances?" It is far more effective to make internal changes first if you want the external things to change.

Finally, you must make sure that what you learn leads to action. There are many who know much, but neglect to apply their knowledge. Do you know people like that? Someone takes every opportunity to learn and grow; they soak up every book, go to every seminar and may even have multiple college degrees, yet do little with it? The only way knowledge has power is when you apply it.

Once you start applying new skills and knowledge, maintain your momentum. There is nothing more useless than learning new skills that can have a dramatic impact on your achievements and then seldom using them. Like a muscle, when knowledge, skills and habits go unused, they dissipate. You've heard the phrase, "use it or lose it." This is why it is important to make a daily commitment to improve and maintain your good habits once you acquire them. Even Michael Jordan understood this. He was at the top of his game and undoubtedly the best player in the world. While filming the movie Space Jam, he had a basketball court built outside the studio, so that during filming breaks he could maintain his skills. This is a commitment to never-ending improvement. It is an example of holding yourself to high standards, which enabled Jordan to form quality habits; making him one of the best players to ever have played the game.

When people continually develop themselves, they become sharper in their thinking. They are equipped with more accurate data that directly corresponds with the quality of decisions they make. They are more likely to come up with effective strategies and solutions for fulfilling their goals. As a result of continually working on themselves, they are more likely to discover what they want and what they are passionate about. Self-improvement leads them not only to achievement, but also to a greater sense of fulfillment.

Today I will do the following to improve myself: ___
_____
_____.

CHAPTER 5

MASTER YOUR THINKING

Law #4

THE QUALITY OF YOUR THINKING—the thoughts and beliefs you entertain, WILL make all the difference. There have been extensive writings on this subject that date back thousands of years. All achievement or defeat is born in the moment of thought. Managing this powerful, yet subtle force, can be your greatest accomplishment in life.

Whatever thoughts you allow to dominate your mind will have a direct impact on what you attract into your life. Like a magnet, each person attracts into his life the people and circumstances that harmonize with his most dominating thoughts. Napoleon Hill made it clear after his classic study of successful people that "thought impulses immediately begin to translate themselves into their physical equivalent, whether those thoughts are voluntary or involuntary."

Emerson said, "We are what we think about all day long." What are you thinking about? If you allow garbage in, garbage is bound to come out. If you let good thoughts dominate your mind, good is likely to come your way. LIKE ATTRACTS LIKE. If your mind is dominated by thoughts of poverty, you will attract poverty into your life. If your mind is dominated by thoughts of anger, you are more likely to be

"A small man is made up of small thoughts"
–Victor Hugo

angry. If your mind is dominated by thoughts of fear, you are more likely to be fearful. If you have pessimistic thoughts, then you are more likely to have a bad attitude. Likewise, if you allow thoughts of small achievement to run rampant through your mind, you will achieve the small things in life. The playwright Victor Hugo said, "A small man is made up of small thoughts." On the other hand, if your mind is dominated by your dreams and goals, then you are bound to attract those dreams and goals into your life.

In his classic book, *As a Man Thinketh*, James Allen writes,

A man does not come to the almshouse or the jail by the tyranny of fate or circumstance, but by the pathway of groveling thoughts and base desires. Nor does a pure-minded man fall suddenly into crime by stress of any mere external force; the criminal thought had long been secretly fostered in the heart, and the hour of opportunity revealed its gathered power. Circumstance does not make the man; it reveals him to himself.

I love this insight because it underscores the truth of the power of thought. There are no accidents. If not managed properly, thoughts can lead to compromise and defeat. They can also lead you to victory.

The same level of thinking that has brought you this far is not going to be enough to take you where you want to go. If I asked: *Who are you? How would you describe yourself? What makes you worthy of your goals? What special attributes or abilities do you process that makes achieving your goals possible?* How would you answer? What are the immediate thoughts that come to your mind? If you want a great life, realize it starts with your level of thinking.

Whether out of worry, fear, or habitual affirmations, much of what the average person thinks about is negative. And at the same time we naively wonder why we feel down, discouraged, and aren't experiencing life the way we would like to. Far too many people have the habit of saying negative phrases to themselves such as, "I can't do that!" "I'm not good enough." "This is the way it's always been." "Things never change!" "My parents haven't achieved anything of great significance." "I don't have any talents." "I can't find a job." "I have a poor memory." Sometimes we even say demeaning statements such as, "I am such an idiot" or "I'm so stupid."

Just when we are about to commit to a goal, we talk ourselves out of it. We question our ability and even our potential. I can remember when just as I was about to speak to a large audience of teachers, a voice inside me asked, "Who do you think you are? You don't have the same level of education as your audience, and besides you're too young." These thoughts not only made me insecure, they almost convinced me to decline the opportunity to speak. These negative thoughts are powerful. Maybe you have had the desire to run for student body office, play sports, or even sign up for drama class. If this negative voice creeps up giving you all the reasons why you can't do it, ignore it and take action to achieve your desired goal.

In her book, *No One Can Take Your Place*, Sheri Dew describes an experience she had when she gave into her self-defeating thoughts. It was a childhood dream of hers to play college basketball. When the date and time arrived she went to the university gym to try out for the 1971 women's basketball team. However, when she opened the gym door to look inside, she saw that girls were already running drills and they were good! At that moment, a little voice said to her, "What are you thinking? You aren't good enough to play ball here! You can't compete with these girls! What has gotten into your head?" She closed the door and gave herself a few moments to regain her composure. However, a few moments turned into hours as she continued pacing the hallway outside the gym telling herself at any moment she would go in. Three hours later, with tryouts over, she left having never gone in. Her dream had been dashed to pieces because she gave into that negative self-talk.

"What are you thinking? You aren't good enough to play ball here!"

Well, 30 years later in the fall of 2001 she was invited to speak to the female athletes of that school. As a part of her talk, for the first time ever she shared the story of pacing the hallway outside the gym in 1971. When she had finished with her remarks, the women's athletic director asked Sheri if that story about never trying out for the team was really true. When Sheri said it was true, the director asked her if she knew that *she* was the coach of the 1971 women's basketball team. Of course Sheri knew that because she had etched the coach's name in her mind ever since and had followed all the successful basketball and volleyball teams she had coached.

The director went on, "Would you like to know something interesting about my 1971 basketball team?" Sheri nodded that she would. The director continued, "In all my years of coaching, it is the only year I was not able to fill my roster, and we played that season one player short. All season I kept searching for one more girl to fill out our team, but I could never find her."

Sheri learned that, "*No one can take your place.* Not

now, not ever."

Unfortunately, many people don't even realize that they are communicating this way. Negative thinking is largely an unconscious process. Often it is difficult to recognize that we are thinking this way, because these mental tapes are constantly playing inside our heads. In many cases they have been playing for years, which makes it difficult to see reality. Our minds become so conditioned that we begin believing it. Therefore, the moment we become aware of self-defeating thoughts pervading our minds, it is vital that we dispel them. More importantly, we must take an active role in discovering these negative thoughts and replace them with useful thoughts.

You can't stop yourself from thinking nor can you always control what thoughts enter your mind, but you can control what you focus and dwell upon. W. Clement Stone said, "The power of thought is the only thing over which any human being has complete unquestionable means of control."

When a negative thought or pattern of thinking enters your mind, don't speak it; set it aside, forget about it, or replace it. When such a thought occurs to you, immediately stop and say to yourself, "Stop!" "Delete." "This is not true." "What I mean is…" Then begin to focus on something positive about the situation. This is not to say that negative things don't happen. They do, but it is more effective to be solution-focused than obstacle-focused. The goal is to prevent yourself from holding onto and replaying negative thoughts.

If you saw a movie you didn't like, would you go back to see it again? Let alone over and over? Of course not! Yet, many people do this inside their minds. They make a mistake or encounter a failure and they play the worst aspect of that experience over and over inside their minds. Remember, you are the creator of your life and whatever thoughts you consistently sow you will also reap.

When you find yourself experiencing negative feelings, it is likely you are thinking similar thoughts. Therefore, stop and change the picture to a more positive one. Change what you focus on in that experience. Choose a new angle. Begin focusing on the benefits of the experience, rather than the pain. Think about it. If you are going to think something over and over, you might as well make it good.

> Change what you are focusing on in that experience.

Bottom line is, all the conditions or experiences we encounter in our lives are created by our thoughts. Many of our outward expressions are the result of our internal feelings. These feelings are caused by our thoughts. Like I've already said, if you think angry thoughts, it will become easier to be angry. If your mind is occupied with thoughts of depression, you are likely to feel depressed. Likewise, if you fill your mind with positive, pleasant thoughts, you will attract positive and pleasant experiences. Your thoughts also have the tendency to reveal themselves in your facial expressions and your overall countenance. Your thoughts are reflected by the way you carry yourself. Have you ever noticed this in others? One person walks around slow and depressed and another walks around with purpose and standing tall. When they walk into the room they light it up. They are smiling and people want to be around them.

If you feel emotional pain in your life from a past failure, defeat, broken relationship, or loss of some kind, it is the result of your thinking, not the circumstance itself. In his book, *Your Erroneous Zones*, Wayne Dyer said, "If you are experiencing an inner discontent as a result of what someone said or did, what you are really saying in that moment is ... 'What that person thinks of me is more important than what I think of myself.'" What people say can affect what we think. You must learn to stand up within yourself.

The most powerful product of thoughts are the beliefs they form. Once we believe something is true, we begin gathering evidence to support that belief, whether true or not. Those beliefs then become our personal truth and reality. Once a belief is formed, rarely do we question its validity. Some are living by limiting beliefs, which are groundless, that they formed twenty or thirty years ago. Don't let this happen to you. Confront your beliefs. Be open to new ideas and different ways of looking at your world. There are multiple sides to most beliefs. You simply have a choice as to which belief you will embrace.

One of my brothers felt depressed and began toying with the idea that anti-depressants were the answer. It didn't make sense. We don't have any cases of depression in our family, but everything he heard from the media provided evidence that taking drugs was the answer to his down moods. When I asked to visit with him, I helped him see how drugs only mask the real cause of the problem. I pointed out a number of people, who he respected in the entertainment industry, who spoke out against these types of drugs and their negative side effects. This new data caused him to re-examine and change his "truth and reality," and from that day forward he has never taken anti-depressants.

Drugs are definitely a discussion for another time, because there are cases when specific drugs are appropriate and necessary. However in this case with my brother, I provided him with a new set of evidence which he *chose* to accept. There was equal evidence to support each side of the argument. And in the end, the only thing that really changed was what he *believed* to be *"true,"* rather than truth itself.

Keep in mind, we all experience highs and lows from time to time. Some days we may feel caught in a funk, loopy, discouraged or sad. This is part of being human.

Whatever you think consistently, you will begin to believe. If you think you're ugly, worthless, and stupid, you may begin to believe it—whether true or not. Likewise, if you think of yourself as beautiful, worthy, and smart, you will eventually believe that too, and begin behaving accordingly.

If you have the habit of saying the phrase, "I can't," then give up the phrase. Go from saying, "I can't..." to adding one word, "I can't...*yet.*" to ultimately saying, "I CAN!" This ugly four letter word, "can't," is extremely powerful in that it is very limiting. If not eliminated, it has the potential to control your life in a negative way.

> This ugly four letter word, "CAN'T", is extremely powerful...

I can still remember the day I eliminated the "I can't" phrase from my vocabulary and I owe a lot of gratitude to a high school senior who taught me a very important lesson. I can remember in the eighth grade going to the high school to participate in sports. One of the sports I chose was track and field, in which I pole-vaulted. On the team was a state champion pole-vaulter who I looked up to. He was popular and always respectful. I never saw him get upset, nor did he ever put anyone down. In many ways I wanted to be like him. Then one day, as I was learning how to pole vault, I became frustrated. All my other teammates seemed to do it effortlessly. After a dozen or more attempts, I became so frustrated that I defiantly threw my pole down on the ground and angrily said, "I can't do it!" I was about to learn a lesson that has impacted every aspect of my life. Immediately upon saying, "I can't do it!" this state champion pole-vaulter calmly walked over to me, looked me directly in the eyes and said, "Can't, never could do it!" He then walked away. I was taken aback, humbled, and openly receptive. In that moment he taught me a very important lesson. One I shall never forget. He encouraged me in that split moment to give up the "I can't…" phrases, because "Can't never could do anything."

Using the word "can't," or any other limiting phrase, systematically shuts off any possibility to succeed. Simply put, our self-talk creates and controls the way we view ourselves, our self-images, beliefs, fears, and comfort zones. As a result, those self-images, beliefs, and comfort zones determine our performance. Thus, our low performance cycles around, confirming and stimulating our self-talk. It becomes an endless loop of reinforcing behavior. Have you ever been asked to give a speech in class? If so, your immediate thought could have been, "I'm a horrible public s peaker." "I always screw up." Consequently, the internal talk creates various pictures that you begin playing in your mind like a movie. These pictures create emotions of fear and nervousness. As a result, when it comes time to open your mouth to speak, your nervousness has caused your hands to become sweaty, your mouth to get dry, and sure enough your mind goes blank. This experience leads you to say to yourself, "See, I knew I couldn't speak in front of people. Who am I fooling?" You have just succeeded in making what is called a "self-fulfilling prophecy". I hope you can clearly see through this example that *you* are ultimately the source of whether you succeed or fail.

Unless you take control of your thinking, you cannot improve your performance. By continually talking or thinking about your present circumstances as they are, you are reinforcing the likelihood of remaining where you are. Albert Einstein said, "The significant problems [you] face cannot be solved by the same level of thinking that created them." You must change your thinking. Instead of focusing on where you are, focus on the future you want to achieve as though you already achieved it. Making this important shift in your thinking will be discussed in chapter 7, *Operating from Your Imagination*.

You may be in the habit of asking lousy questions, like: "Why do I always screw up?" "Why don't things ever work out for me?" You fall into the trap of asking these lousy questions and guess what happens? Your mind does exactly what it is designed to do, which is to come up with answers. As a result of these lousy questions, you get lousy answers. You've heard the phrase, "Ask and ye shall receive." Has it ever dawned on you that by simply changing the questions you ask yourself, you can change your thinking and thereby the results you attract into your life? For example, you could change "Why do I always screw up?" to "What must I do better next time?" Or change from, "Why don't things ever work out for me?" to "What must I do differently to ensure succeeding at this task in the future?"

Your thoughts can either create fear or they

can create confidence. Your thoughts can create pain or they can create pleasure. Your thoughts can lead you to take action or they can drive you to withdraw and even give up. Likewise, the philosopher Virgil once said, "They can because they think they can."

How do you control your thoughts? Make certain that whatever you allow into your mind is healthy and positive. It is vital that you begin today by engaging in uplifting conversations with yourself and others. Be wise with your television and news intake. Be aware of the books and magazines that you read. Do they uplift you? Do they inspire you to stretch and grow for the better? Or, do they gossip and speak ill of others? Each one of these activities, if not cautiously managed, can dramatically affect you. You may not see signs of their existence today or tomorrow, but sooner or later they will begin affecting your behavior and performance.

Although you may be filling your mind with uplifting material, destructive thoughts still have a way of surfacing. A simple strategy I have found to reduce the impact of such thoughts is to immediately change your physiology once you become aware of the negative thought. When speaking of physiology I am referring to the way a person uses or carries his physical body. From the way you stand, sit, use your facial expressions and more, all play a significant role in what you experience internally. If a self-defeating thought enters your mind, stand up, take a walk, or simply engage in an activity that will distract you from dwelling on the thought. This immediately disrupts the pattern of negative thinking and helps prevent the thought from taking root.

Therefore, get in the habit of changing your physiology to support the desired positive thought you plan to focus on. When you put your body in a position that reflects a confident and calm person, thoughts have the tendency of internally experiencing the feelings of confidence and calmness. Use this strategy to redirect and refocus your thoughts. If you are nervous about asking someone on a date or making a great impression on a job interview imagine yourself succeeding and simultaneously put your body in the corresponding position as if it were true. You will be amazed with the impact this small change can have.

Distracting yourself may be effective for the moment, but will not always serve as an effective long-term solution. Therefore, another useful strategy is to get in the habit of recognizing destructive thinking when it arises and stop it immediately. In a disciplined way, cut off its nourishment. If negative or self-defeating thoughts persist, then evaluate their accuracy. Start looking for evidence that will make the negative thought inaccurate. Often these thoughts are groundless and unsupported in reality.

Once you have moved your body and begun

focusing on something new, look at your goals and say to yourself—*It's possible!* You must not only think in terms of general possibility, but also begin thinking it is possible for you personally. Begin seeing yourself achieving what you want and allow that picture to dominate your mind.

Get in the habit of standing up inside yourself every day and convincing yourself that you have what it takes–regardless of your current level of performance. Every day you must convince yourself that you are unstoppable. Convince yourself every day that your goals have value. It is vital that what you think and say to yourself reflects your expectation that your goals can and will be accomplished. These are the dominating thoughts you want occupying your mind.

As you alter your thoughts toward people, they will in turn alter their thoughts toward you. If you alter your thoughts about your world, your world will change to be consistent with those thoughts. If you will alter your thoughts away from those things you fear, the fear will dissipate. There is an African proverb that states, "If there is no enemy within, the enemy on the outside can do us no harm." If you alter the way you think about yourself, this will alter what you attract into your day-to-day experience.

Any seed nourished will eventually bear fruit, good or bad. What fruit are you yielding? What are you thinking? Whatever you think about consistently, you will eventually attract. Think wisely!

What are the random negative thoughts or beliefs I will begin to control or eliminate?_____

_____

_____

_____.

What are the positive thoughts I will replace them with? _____

_____

_____

_____.

CHAPTER 6

WHAT DO YOU WANT?

Law #5

FIVE YEARS FROM NOW YOU ARE GOING to arrive. The question is where? If you don't know what you want, how will you ever recognize it when you have it? The truth is, if you don't know what you want, you are likely to wind up getting nowhere very quickly. Without direction, it's just a matter of time before you are working at a job or staying in a relationship you dislike, or simply living an unfulfilling life.

Most people are wandering through life without direction. They are not reaching for worthwhile goals. They mingle through life like spectators, watching the game on the field. Yet, if you saw an achiever and asked how he managed to achieve, I doubt he would say, "Well—I just started wandering around and ended up here." No, you have to be able to name it in order to claim it.

Achievers know exactly what they want and *consistently move toward it.* It is amazing how many people don't know what they want in life. Among the many people I have worked with, I am amazed at how many people go from one day to the next not knowing where they really intend to go. And unfortunately it becomes a pattern of living. In the beginning it starts by thinking, "Eventually, I'll figure out what I want." "I'll start tomorrow." "Someday I'll decide what I want…" If you are thinking this—STOP!

> Achievers know exactly what they want…

I mentioned earlier that you attract based on the sum total of your dominating thoughts. Once you are clear about what you want, the universe works day and night to help attract it into your life. Opportunities will show up out of nowhere. You'll begin recognizing things that you otherwise would have never noticed before. In many cases, you will realize that these opportunities were right in front of you the whole time; you were simply filtering them out of your awareness.

Maxwell Maltz described this power as a servo-mechanism, "an automatic goal-seeking machine which 'steers' its way to a target or a goal by use of feedback data and stored information automatically correcting course when necessary." Our mind has a way of focusing on what we want and filtering out information that is not important to us—it is a survival mechanism.

If you were unable to filter out all the data that is constantly bombarding your brain, you would go crazy. For example, place this book down for a moment and do the following exercise. Become still and notice all the sounds that are around you. You may notice sounds you were not aware of a minute ago. Maybe you hear the air-conditioning, people shifting or walking around. Maybe you notice your breathing or cars driving outside your home. You have a built-in system that tunes out what is not important to you. Therefore, if you are not careful you may unknowingly tune out the opportunities and resources that can help you to achieve your goals.

The bottom line is, if you are unclear about what you want out of life, even if opportunities arise, they will simply go unnoticed. You will unknowingly overlook the exact resources that could help you successfully get from point A to point B. On the other hand, when you are clear about what you want to achieve, you will notice the slightest opportunity that can lead to the accomplishment of your goal. This is called the "law of attraction"—a combination of knowing what you want and directing your thoughts accordingly. When I worked with Tony Robbins, it wasn't by accident. When I wrote my first script for a motion picture, or helped build two multi million-dollar companies, it wasn't by accident. When I look at all the opportunities that have revealed themselves to me over the years, I am convinced that they came as a result of clearly knowing what I wanted and living my life in such a way that made those goals attainable.

For years I've wanted to write a book. Then one night I was listening to an audiotape of another best selling author and motivational speaker, Charles "Tremendous" Jones. While listening, I noticed a phone number on the cassette tape label. The set of tapes must have been thirty years old and most people wouldn't have given the number another thought. However, I did. I thought to myself, "I wonder if this phone number is still active and if so, I wonder what state it leads to?" It was eleven o'clock at night, I dialed the phone number and it began ringing. Then, just as I was about to hang up, someone answered. The voice on the other end said, "Who is this?"

In response I said, "Who is this?" After a short pause I got the feeling I'd better tell him, so I gave him my name.

I then asked, "May I ask with whom I am speaking?"

I can still remember him saying in a low voice, "This is Charles 'Tremendous' Jones."

Surprised I said, "You've got to be kidding me! This is the Charles 'Tremendous' Jones?"

He said, "That's me!"

I asked, "Where do you live?"

He said, "Pennsylvania."

I quickly apologized. "Please tell me I didn't wake you up."

"Oh, no," he replied.

I said, "It's one o'clock in the morning," and I inquired why he was up at that hour. He proceeded to tell me he was reading one of his many books.

I remember visiting with him for probably forty minutes or so as he shared some advice about writing a book. Toward the end of our discussion he asked me for my fax number. When I awoke the next morning I was excited to see he had sent me a twenty-page fax with more advice. On the cover page was a handwritten note that I still cherish today. Among other things it read, "I'm looking forward to reading your manuscript." This experience was not simply a coincidence!

Eight months later I was reading a book called, *The Joy of Failure* by Wayne Allyn Root. It was a Saturday morning about 9:00 a.m. when I completed the book and noticed a phone number on the last page. Would it surprise you if I told you that I dialed the number? Would it surprise you if I said that Mr. Root answered the phone? Well, that is exactly what happened. That morning he was in his office all alone when he answered the phone. We talked for about ten minutes and he shared his strategy for writing a book.

He said, "If you will write an hour and a half each day, by the end of a year you will have written a two-hundred-page book." Coincidence? No!

Eight months later I was in Southern California when I was reminded that the renowned author and trainer Brian Tracy's office was near where I was staying. After downloading the directions from the Internet, I drove to his office. He travels frequently, so I knew it was unlikely he would be there, but I wanted a tour of his office. When I arrived, the secretary was puzzled by my request. She said she had never been asked to give a tour before, and that she would need to speak to her supervisor. When she stood up to leave, I asked her if Brian Tracy ever came in the office.

She said, "Normally, no."

The word "normally" came off her lips a little hesitantly, so I inquired about her use of the word.

She responded, "Typically, when Mr. Tracy comes into town from being on the road, he works out of his home in an effort to spend as much time as possible with his family."

However, she did say that he happened to be in the office that particular morning. Upon hearing that information, I immediately asked if I could meet Mr. Tracy. She said she wasn't sure and left to ask her supervisor.

Let me stop right here and say that when you are clear about what you want, it is important to impress the mind with as much detail as possible. It is important to create a very clear picture of what you want. I thought having a tour of his office might provide me with supportive detail. I wanted to see what "my future office" might look like. The secretary left the foyer, and two minutes later the president walked up and asked how he could help me. I explained that I wanted a tour of the office and explained why.

I continued, "Since Mr. Tracy is in the office I'd like to meet him, too." He told me he would see what he could do.

Two minutes later I remember looking down the office hallway from the foyer watching Brian Tracy walk right toward me. I'll never forget the sight. Six-feet tall, white hair, wearing jeans, flip-flops, Hawaiian shirt, and a big smile.

He walked right up to me with his hand out to shake mine and said, "Hi, I'm Brian Tracy."

I said, "Hi, I'm TJ Hoisington."

We visited for a few minutes, and he proceeded to give me a tour of his office. Once we made it back to the foyer, and just as our visit came to a close, I remembered the words of a speaker who said, "Always act when the emotion is high."

I told Mr. Tracy that I recently started writing a book and asked if he would be willing to read the manuscript and write an endorsement.

He thought for a moment and said, "I'd be happy to. Send me the first chapter and the table of contents..."

Not only did Brian Tracy endorse the original "*If You Think You Can!*" book for adults, but also Wayne Allyn Root and Charles "Tremendous" Jones lent their support. Not only was I committed to working on myself, but also I was committed to my goal.

Again, were these experiences simply coincidence or luck? Definitely not. In fact, the story doesn't even stop there. A few months later I happened to be at the right place at the right time and met Jack Canfield, coauthor of the best-selling book, "*Chicken Soup for the Soul.*" Not only did Jack endorse the original "*If You Think You Can!*," he spent time giving me five pointers that could make my book a success.

These experiences were neither coincidence nor luck. (Branch Rickey, the Brooklyn Dodgers' general manager often remarked, "*Luck is the residue of design.*") They were the result of a clear vision and commitment to achieving what I wanted. My clear goals influenced my thoughts and decisions that enabled me to gravitate toward opportunities that supported my desires. The same can happen for you.

> "Luck is the
> residue of
> design."
> *—Branch Rickey*

What is even more amazing is that initially you don't need to know *how* you are going to reach your goal. I found that if you will first become clear about what you want and why you want it, then *how* to achieve it will reveal itself at the appropriate time. Your reasons come first and answers come second. Once you are clear and committed about what you want, the law of attraction is set in motion.

Am I saying that doing the research and having a strategy is not important? Of course not! There is a time when having a strategy and plan is vitally important, but initially it is more important to know *what* you want, *why* you want it, and then make a commitment that you are going to achieve it. Many people spend so much energy worrying about "how" to do something that it becomes overwhelming and they decide not to go after the goal at all. Some people suffer from "analysis paralysis," a condition in which people over analyze, yet *do* nothing (or do little to make their dreams come true). The law dictates that once you decide *what* you want and *why* you want something, the "how" will make itself known at the appropriate time.

Another important aspect of knowing what you want is: Be sure you dwell on what you want rather than dwelling on what you don't want. For example, if I told you, "Don't picture yourself standing on the top of the Empire State building wearing a pink tutu", I'll bet you couldn't help but have that exact picture flash before your minds eye.

I'll often ask people what they want out of life or out of a particular experience, and they immediately begin explaining what they *don't* want. They focus on the fear or the disappointment of failure, rather than focusing on the reward of taking the risk. Whatever image you hold in your mind will begin to reflect itself in your world.

It is also important to be specific. To say you want a boyfriend or girlfriend, to be accepted into a good college, or drive a cool car, is not enough to start attracting them. Instead, make the picture so vivid that you can describe in detail what you want. Describe the car type and any unique features of the car. What about the color? Is price important to you? This much detail and more is necessary. What will it look and feel like to achieve the goal? And most importantly, why is it important to you? What are all the benefits? And then write each answer down on paper. This level of clarity will enable you to effectively hone in on your dreams.

The most important part of getting what you want is to begin dreaming about it. Dreaming creates a burning desire that turns possibility into reality. Imagine if money, time, talent, and education were not obstacles. What would you go after? What are you passionate about? What would keep you up late at night and get you up early in the morning? What if you knew you couldn't fail? What would it be? George Burns, the American comedian, actor, singer, and writer, once said, "*I would rather fail at something that I love than succeed at something I hate.*" What would you do if you won a million dollars? What if you unexpectedly learned that you only had six months to live? Again, what would it be?

> Imagine if money, time, talent, and education were NOT obstacles.

It is vital that you take time out—spend time in solitude if necessary—and decide what you would love to do above all else. Go ahead lie down on your bed, stare at the ceiling and daydream. Let your mind go wild. No, I'm not talking about wanting the latest style of clothes or a new cell phone. I'm talking about what really inspires you? Reflect on what interests you have. What comes easily to you and simultaneously gives you a sense of satisfaction? These answers should serve as clues to discovering what you want.

Think BIG by making a list of 20 things you would love to do. Then think of ways you can design your life around those 20 things. If you find it somewhat difficult to come up with what you want, begin asking yourself the question, "If I did know, what would it be?" Ask this over and over and your brain will eventually start giving you the answers. Then write those thoughts down on a piece of paper. Keep in mind that whatever you like doing, there is a way to make a living at it.

If you find yourself at any point where you think you know what you want, yet you're not really sure, I suggest that you take some small action toward that desired goal. This allows you to get a "taste" of the particular goal. If the "taste" is satisfactory and you get the impression this is something that may work for you—be decisive and go for it!

There is no such thing as an unrealistic goal. Your time frame, current condition, or strategy may be ineffective or unrealistic, like a three-hundred-pound jockey expecting to win a race. Or entering the ring to box Muhammad Ali— some things are ridiculously insane. But for the most part, the goals you choose will be attainable. Granted, your goals may require that you stretch, grow, and improve. Some goals will require that you develop new skills. Others will require that you change your environment. Whatever it is, there are some things out of your control, but there are many things that are within your control. Choose to occupy your mind with only those things you can control. All too often, people kill a goal before they ever have a chance of letting it take shape because they believe it is too far out of our reach. However, I like the advice Price Pritchett once gave, "If you are going to doubt something, doubt your limits."

Mortimer Adler said, "If you don't strive for the high things in life, you'll settle for the low." My good friend Bob Moawad says, "Most people don't aim too high and miss, they aim too low and hit." Remember, the size of your goals determines the size of your results—so dream BIG! Dream bigger than you ever thought you could dream! Big dreams attract big people. Big dreams attract big opportunities. Big dreams create big results. When you mix big dreams with commitment, unforeseen things will happen that will help turn your goals into reality.

> Dream bigger than you ever thought you could dream.

Never let it be said of you that you didn't know what you wanted. Never let it be said that you lived other people's dreams and goals. Decide *today* that you will become clear about what you want and make a commitment to achieve it.

What activities do I currently engage that create satisfaction and enjoyment? _____

_____

_____

_____

_____

_____.

What activities can you imagine doing in the future that would create satisfaction and enjoyment? _____

_____

_____

_____.

I am passionate and committed about what? If money, time, resources, or opportunity were not an obstacle—what would I choose to do? _____

_____

_____

_____.

CHAPTER 7

OPERATING FROM YOUR IMAGINATION

Law #6

YOUR IMAGINATION IS A MAJOR SOURCE of desire and motivation. It is the primary source to creating change and it is the incubator of all ideas that eventually make their way into reality. Before any song is ever sung, building is ever erected, an invention ever created, or change ever made, it is first breathed into life in someone's imagination. In the *Laws of Success*, Napoleon Hill taught, "All achievement starts in the imagination before it is ever realized in the physical form."

Achievers get what they want because they utilize the power of their imagination in a very resourceful way. It is the imagination that takes the invisible and makes it visible.

This was the case of Fred Smith, who gave birth to the idea of the overnight shipping business now known as FedEx. Using his imagination, Walt Disney created an empire in such a way that no one had done before. Conrad Hilton of Hilton Hotels imagined himself owning a hotel long before he ever bought one. The same is true with people like Bill Gates, who created Microsoft, or Ray Kroc, who through McDonalds, created the model for fast food restaurants. They and thousands of others all started with an idea and used their imaginations to turn their ideas into reality.

Often, these individuals didn't have special education or knowledge. They used their imaginations in such ways that they made new combinations with the knowledge they already possessed. Look at Baskin and Robbins, two brothers who had a dream of starting a business. What was their successful idea? They simply opened a shop serving ice cream with thirty-one different flavors. Baskin-Robbins' success wasn't the result of a vast knowledge base or being privy to some think-tank collection of cutting-edge ideas. Rather, they simply used their imaginations in a creative way.

The entire South was changed by the power of one man's use of his imagination. While watching his cat trying to claw a chicken through the walls of its coop, Eli Whitney noticed that the cat was only successful at getting a paw full of feathers. Thus, an idea was born. He imagined an iron claw pulling cotton from a cotton plant. As a result, Eli invented a revolutionary machine: the cotton gin. Again, the power of the imagination.

After a meeting with the founder of Polaroid Corporation, Steve Jobs, the founder of Apple Computer and the music Ipod said, "It's like when I walk in a room, and I want to talk about a product that hasn't even been invented yet. I can see the product as if it is sitting there, right in the center of the table. What I've got to do is materialize it and bring it to life." Unbelievable!

Most people are living by the belief, "I'll believe it when I see it." On the other hand, achievers understand "When they believe it, then they'll see it." They understand that, if they can imagine it, it is likely they can achieve it. Outlandish or not, if you can "see" it, then believe in it and begin finding reasons and means that will turn the thought into reality.

> "When you believe it, than you'll see it."

Such was the case with actor Jim Carrey before he ever made it to the big screen. Carrey believed in his dream so much that "as a gesture of faith, he wrote himself a check for ten million dollars for 'acting services rendered' and carried it in his wallet for seven years." As a result of his imagination and his belief in his internal picture, he literally began to structure his life around that desire. Operating from his imagination enabled him to "see" what he wanted to have happen in his mind's eye as though he had already achieved it.

Jim Carrey himself said:

I've always believed in magic. When I wasn't doing anything in this town, I'd go up every night, sit on Mulholland Drive, look out at the city, stretch out my arms, and say, "Everybody wants to work with me. I'm a really good actor. I have all kinds of great movie offers." I'd just repeat these things over and over, literally convincing myself that I had a couple of movies lined up. I'd drive down that hill, ready to take the world on, going, "Movie offers are out there for me, I just don't hear them yet." It was like total affirmations, antidotes to the stuff that stems from my family background.

Consciously operating from your imagination is a necessary habit to acquire. Begin thinking in terms of "fake it until you make it" or "acting as if" you have already achieved your goals. Charles F. Kettering, inventor with over 140 patents and honorary doctorates from nearly 30 universities said, "Believe and *act as if* it were impossible to fail." Make your goals as internally vivid as possible. What does it look like? What does it feel like? How did you achieve it—as if you already had? What steps did you take that led to success?

In his book, *Golf My Way*, Jack Nicklaus writes, "First I see the ball where I want it to finish, nice and white and sitting up there on the bright green grass. Then, I see the scene quickly change and I see the ball going there, its path, trajectory, and shape, even its behavior on the landing. Then there is sort of a fade out and the next scene shows me making the kind of swing that will turn the previous images into reality." Jack started with the end in mind, as though he already accomplished his desired result.

Unfortunately, most people perform based on memories of their past performances, thus allowing their past performances, good or bad, to govern future performances. They think in terms of "I've never done it before, what makes me think I can do it now?" Because of this type of thinking, if unsuccessful past attempts are dominating our minds, then we will continue to perform accordingly.

However, people who achieve greatness have made a definite habit of operating from their imagination. They choose to use it as a tool. They understand they cannot drive forward through life while looking through the rearview mirror.

Imagine playing golf and never scoring below ninety. Then imagine taking a seven-year break, and the next time you played you shot a seventy-four. I'm sure you would agree, assuming you understand golf and the lower the score the better, that would be remarkable. Well, that is exactly what happened to Major Nesmeth. Years ago he was sent to Vietnam during the Vietnam War and was eventually captured. He then spent the next seven years in a small cage that was only four feet by four feet in and only four and a half feet tall. To prevent himself from going insane he spent his waking moments imagining himself playing golf. Seven days a week he imagined everything from the clothes he wore, to his grip and swing. He imagined the ball flying through the air and landing precisely where he wanted it to land. Day after day he played the perfect game inside his mind's eye, while in reality he was restricted and suffering. By the time he was released from prison seven years later, his imagined game had become such a part of him that rather than picking up where he had left off, he dramatically improved his game—by nothing more than his imagination.

Had he repeatedly imagined his past performance of never scoring below ninety during those seven years, his game would have remained the same. Instead, he imagined a better game, and conditioned it into his mind, which allowed his physical performance to harmonize with his internal picture.

Before I ever gave my first speech, I rehearsed it many times in my mind's eye. I then relied heavily on the successful image I had created. Although I inevitably made mistakes, I kept my focus on the successful performances and then adjusted accordingly. Eventually, through mentally reviewing the internal picture that I held for myself, I became exactly who I am today. The same will work in your life. If there is an area in your life that you would like to improve, then begin imagining your behavior as though you have already improved in that area. What does it look like? What does it feel like? How do others perceive you? Imagine it as vividly as possible and it will start to affect your performance. Harvard University researchers found those students who visualized in advance, performed tasks with almost 100% accuracy. Students who did not visualize performing their tasks in advance, achieved only 55% accuracy.

A powerful, yet widely accepted truth about the mind is that it cannot always tell the difference between something that is vividly imagined and that which actually happens. Some psychologists claim that seven hours of visualization is equal to one hour of actual experience. Other psychologists suggest that visualizing accompanied with emotion is

> The mind cannot always tell the difference...

sixty times as powerful as a real event. Have you ever had the experience of lying in bed and being frightened by an object in the room, only to turn on the lights or wake up the next morning to find that it was only a familiar object out of place? Or maybe you were awoken by a dream. Although in reality the cause of your fear was inaccurate, it sure felt real, didn't it?

Imagine taking a lemon and cutting it into two pieces. You pick up one half of the lemon, position it over your mouth and squeeze it until lemon juice falls onto your tongue. If you imagine this vividly enough you will have felt some physical sensation. The cause of the sensation had little to do with reality, yet it still had a sensory impact.

Have you ever been driving down the road or even sitting in class when the thought of a past experience popped into your mind that made you feel embarrassed, fearful, or even depressed? We have already talked about thoughts and the same is true with the pictures you play in your imagination—they become true to you. We must be careful what we allow to take shape inside our minds. Anything that is continually repeated or imagined will eventually be accepted as your personal truth and reality.

How does this apply to you? If you can't see yourself getting the job, you probably won't. The same is true with owning your own business or taking a risk. What about American Idol? If you can't imagine yourself successfully performing you probably won't. If you can't see yourself creating the result you desire, it is unlikely you will make progress in that area.

If you picture and say, "I can't," "I feel depressed," "I'll never be able to afford that," "I'm ugly," then your mind will take you at your word. Learning to operate from your imagination is one of the strongest tools you have to produce the results you want.

For just a moment, allow me to be a little technical. There are two primary purposes of the subconscious mind. The first is to store information. It stores everything you have ever seen, heard, smelt, and felt with emotion. It stores all your life experiences, knowledge, skills, self-images, even your personality. This data is stored in the subconscious mind as your "truth and reality." The second purpose of the subconscious mind is to "make you act like you." Its purpose is to keep you behaving in harmony with the information it has gathered and stored over the years. In other words, the subconscious mind compels you to act and behave in alignment with your dominate "reality."

Joseph Murphy in his book, *The Power of the Subconscious Mind* uses the analogy of the captain and the engine of the ship to illustrate the differing roles of the conscious and subconscious minds. He explains that the captain of the ship is like unto the conscious mind. The captain is the master of the ship, he is in charge. He controls all the instruments, gauges, boilers, and the crew in the engine room. Ultimately, the captain controls the direction of the ship. Below the deck is the engine room; this represents the subconscious mind. It is the source of power, the very power that moves the ship from one location to the other. He explains that if the captain on the bridge of the ship decided to send orders to the engine room to turn the ship onto the rocks, the crew would simply follow his orders. The crew in the engine room cannot see where the captain is leading them. There are no windows. They just know he is in charge. Likewise, the engine doesn't talk back. It simply carries out whatever the captain commands. The subconscious mind works in the same fashion. It takes whatever information is given it by the conscious mind, and goes to work to make it reality.

How does this affect you? Simply, whatever phrases you repeatedly speak or pictures you imagine will eventually be imprinted in your subconscious mind and be accepted as "truth and reality." Once the information has been received, it is the job of the subconscious mind to make you act like you; meaning it causes you to act, behave, and perform in harmony with your dominate thoughts and beliefs. In other words, if you continue to say phrases such as, "I can't" or "I always screw up" or "I'll never get the dream job" or "I'll *never* make my dreams come true," the subconscious mind will see to it that the task "can't" be done or that you will not be in a position to realize your dreams. Eliminate those negative phrases and replace them with positive ones!

"I always screw up."
"I'll never get my dream job."

Henry Ford must have known what he was talking about when he said, "Whether you think you can or think you can't, you are right." Why? Once we form a belief, we immediately start gathering evidence to support the belief, whether it is positive or negative. Therefore, begin consciously creating the pictures you want to become your future reality. This is also one way to stretch your comfort zone; by bombarding your subconscious mind with new thoughts and images that reflect what you want, rather than what you don't want.

Take a few minutes every day to imagine and be creative. Practice this principle. It may not come naturally, but with practice your ability will increase. Ralph Waldo Emerson said, "That which we persist in doing becomes easier—not that the nature of the task has changed, but our ability to do it has increased." Just like the first time you drove your car.

When you fear something and yet desire to feel calm and collected, simply change your fearful internal picture to a calm and centered picture in spite of your circumstances. Are you focusing too heavily on your past, or are you anticipating failure in the future? Change your internal channel and refocus your thoughts to a picture that creates calmness.

Because the pictures we imagine are the primary cause of fear, here is a simple strategy you can use to overcome fear: Allow yourself for a moment to imagine the scenario that is creating the fear. Then switch the picture and see yourself in that same scenario performing successfully. Repeat this newly constructed picture as many times as needed, until it is conditioned. While rehearsing this successful picture from beginning to end as vividly as possible, simultaneously say to yourself those phrases and statements that you would say if you were truly confident and able. "Good things happen to me." "I'm excited and ready." "I'm unstoppable!" and "I can do it!" You may even decide to listen to energetic and upbeat music that will assist you with getting yourself into a confident state of mind.

By imagining a successful outcome, you not only reduce the negative emotions associated with taking action, but you can also eliminate them. Allow yourself to feel elated by your imagined successful performance as you play it over and over. In fact, play the successful performance over and over a minimum of ten times to condition it into your mind. Then, once in a resourceful and confident state of mind, be sure to act. Taking action in that moment will greatly contribute to conquering your fear.

You can even use your imagination to change a behavior. If there are triggers in your environment that lead you to anger, depression, or discouragement, then use your imagination to overcome them.

Whether you are learning a new skill, changing an area of your life, or working on a specific goal, it is necessary to rehearse and experience what you want to have happen ahead of time. Brian Tracy said, "Winners make a habit of manufacturing their own positive expectations in advance of the event, expecting the very best to come out of their efforts, even though they have no information on which to base it."

Dreams are formed in the imagination and since "life is but a dream" dream on.

Today I will begin operating from my imagination to improve in this specific area of my performance: _____

_____

_____

_____.

CHAPTER 8

. . . .

ACTION: THE WINNERS EDGE

Law #7

WHAT IS THE MAJOR DIFFERENCE BETWEEN the successful and the unsuccessful? Albert E.N. Gray said, "The common denominator is that the successful were willing to do the things that the unsuccessful people were not willing to do." Action is what separates wishful thinkers from those who turn their ideas and goals into reality. You can have all the dreams, inspiration, knowledge, and even talent in the world, but if you don't take action, nothing will happen.

Inspiration must lead to action. In a very real sense, operating from your imagination goes beyond dreaming and wishful thinking—it leads the committed person to take the necessary action that will turn the internal picture into reality. Simply by being clear about what you want will put you in the top 5% of high achievers. In order to reach the top 1% all you have to do is decide on specific action steps and then begin taking action.

In 2003, I had a wild idea for a movie script. Yes! You heard it right. An idea for a big motion picture. It all started one night when I decided to have movie night with my then five-year-old and three-year-old sons. I pulled out the 1960 Disney version of Swiss Family Robinson and began watching. My son's eyes were glued to the television screen. As I sat with them each at my side, with popcorn in a bowl, it didn't take long before the thought crossed my mind, "I wonder why a sequel to this popular movie had never been written or produced?" Somehow it had slipped under the Hollywood radar. I couldn't get the idea out of my head. I had never thought of myself as a screenwriter. And although it was a big stretch, I thought—why not! I've always believed in possibilities.

Then later that night at 1 o'clock in the morning, I awoke with the sequel in my mind's eye. I could see it! After debating for a minute or two on whether I should get out of bed or simply wait for the morning to write down my initial ideas, I decided to get out of bed and begin writing.

Over the next days and months, did I ever have doubts? Yes—of course. There were times when that negative voice would enter my thinking and try to convince me I was incapable. There were times when I felt overwhelmed. But the idea was clear, and I was going to live the principles I teach, even if the goal seemed to be a far reach.

I typed throughout that first night. The next day I continued thinking about it. A few days later I even called some friends together and told them about my idea. They all thought the story was great and that it definitely had potential, but they proceeded to remind me that none of us had ever written a movie script before. They said, "We don't know where to start." "We don't have any contacts." "There must be an easier way."

> What separated the achievers from thousands of unachievers?

After inviting them to leave, I was reminded that there were many people before the Wright brothers who had envisioned flying, yet did little about it. Many people before Alexander Graham Bell thought about the concept of the telephone, yet no one ever successfully turned the idea into reality. Others had thoughts and ambitions about cars before Henry Ford began massively producing them. What made them different? What separated the achievers from the thousands of underachievers? The answer is quite simple—*action*.

Have you ever had an idea for something that you knew people would like, and then walked into a store and noticed it on the shelf or seen it online? What was the difference between you and that other person? The difference was, that person took action on his idea.

Time and time again I read about people who didn't wait around for opportunities to simply show up. Instead, when all else failed, they created them. In the 1970s, Sylvester Stallone, the American actor, screenwriter, producer, and director, was financially broke after writing several scripts that were all rejected. But he didn't give up; he didn't resign himself to the bleak outlook that his goals as a writer and actor were not possible. Instead he continued taking action and looking for his break. Then one night in 1975 he found himself inspired by watching a boxing match between Chuck Wepner and Muhammad Ali. Although the odds were greatly against Wepner, thirty-to-one, he surprisingly withstood fifteen beating rounds, before being defeated by the great Muhammad Ali. Returning home, Stallone immediately began writing the script that would not only change his life, but became the mega-hit movie *Rocky*. Written in three days, created on a budget of one million dollars, and filmed in twenty-eight days, *Rocky* is one of the biggest successes in the film industry, grossing over $100 million.

Nia Vardalos was another person who was tired of casting agents telling her "Next!" So she created a one-woman play that eventually led to the successful movie My Big Fat Greek Wedding. True achievers make it a habit of not sitting around waiting for their break; they create it. They take action! Howard Schultz, Starbucks Coffee's founder and chairman asks, "What distinguishes the talented person who makes it from the person who has even more talent but doesn't get ahead? Part of what constitutes success is timing and chance. But most of us have to create our own opportunities and be prepared to jump when we see the big one others can't see."

In my case, I had never written a movie script before. I didn't know the format or rules for properly writing one, but I did believe it was possible to learn. I was also willing to take necessary action. I thought to myself, either I am going to write the script or sooner or later someone else will. So, I went to the local bookstore and purchased three books on screenwriting. After reading each of them, I began to write. When I was on the road traveling to various speaking engagements, I would write. I wrote in the hotel rooms, and even late at night at home after my family went to bed. I was consumed. A few months and one hundred and twenty-five pages later, the script was finished.

> Life truly does, "REWARD ACTION."

As of today, I have taken the additional step to turn the one hundred and twenty-five-page script into a four hundred page novel titled, "*Return to Robinson Island.*" It is the *first Swiss Family Robinson sequel in over one hundred years* and is now available! If you are looking for an adventurous and entertaining read filled with love, betrayal, and survival, this is a book for you! For more information, visit: **www.SwissFamilyReturns.com**

We are all afforded a certain number of opportunities

in life and we must act on them when they come. Are there better and more qualified writers than I? Absolutely, but I looked out and saw people who were doing it and thought to myself, "They aren't any smarter than I am." Sure, there were days when the ideas wouldn't come and I had severe writer's block. However, one day at a time, I operated from my imagination, taking one step at a time.

Every day I imagined the story I was writing and also what the completion would look like. I thought of all the opportunities that would surely come my way as a result. I imagined the doors that would open which would allow me to have greater impact on larger numbers of people worldwide. I even imagined someday walking down the Hollywood red carpet. Even if writers don't walk down the red carpet, it sure felt exciting. Using my imagination in this way enabled me to take an almost overwhelming task at times and find joy in it.

I made the decision that I would no longer talk about my idea. I was going to put my action where my mouth was. I was going to be a doer and not a talker. I had gone from being interested in the idea to being committed to it. Does this take courage? Yes. Will there be some who will doubt you – even mock you? Yes. Are you going to get resistance from people in your life – even your friends? Yes. Will there be times when you feel you don't have what it takes? Yes. Will you experience fear? Yes–of course. But

Courage is NOT the absence of FEAR!

remember it takes a bigger man or women to act despite the fear. This is called having courage. Courage is not the absence of fear, it is the ability to feel the fear and do it anyway. Be a risk taker.

"Action" is how my oldest son was able to break three Washington State High School Football Records his junior year of high school. As a young man he, like thousands of other youth, wanted to play football. His inner goal is to play college football, and he is on track to make that happen. As a running back, he broke the "all season rushing record" with 2,929 rushing yards in ten games. He also broke the state record for the most rushing yards in a single game with 573 yards. And he set the record for most touchdowns in a single game with nine touchdowns and three, two-point conversions.

How was he able to do it? Answer: Action! Growing up, I would tell him that natural talent can only take you so far. I would say, "Bryce if you want to be the best and even play college football, you'll have to pay the price - particularly when no one is watching. Discipline is the key!"

On his own time, during the spring and summer, five days a week, Bryce would train. He would run with the sled with 45-pound weights loaded on top. He did speed and footwork with the speed-latter. He lifted weights. Bryce also invested time and money to work with a private trainer. He would do all this when other athletes high high hopes were likely playing video games or watching television—*merely wishing for their dreams to come true.* Bryce paid the price, and he was rewarded. Who knows what the future has in store, but as I write this book, colleges have been scouting him, and it's been a fun ride thus far.

A young man was playing the piano late one night in a club when a patron who had been drinking came up to him and asked him to sing. The man was a regular in the club and spent a lot of money there. He told the pianist that he didn't come to the club to hear someone only playing the piano—he wanted to hear singing. The pianist looked up at him and said he was not a singer, and that he only played the piano. Consequently, the man became upset and walked over to the bartender expressing his desire to hear singing. He told the bartender that if he didn't start hearing some singing, he and his friends would leave. Immediately, the bartender walked over to this young man playing the piano and told him that if he didn't start singing, he would be fired and forced to go out and find a new job somewhere else. Although he didn't see himself as a singer, he sang anyway. And no one ever sang the song "Sweet Lorraine" like Nat King Cole. That night was not only an eye-opener for Nat, it was a breakthrough. It had awakened the greatness he possessed within. After patrons made continual requests to hear him sing, someone at Decca Records heard his rendition and immediately wanted to sign him to the label. The rest is history.

There will be times when the ability to take action

will require you to face your fears and inadequacies. At times there will be a voice inside that will try to convince you your dream is not possible. But like Nat King Cole, sometimes it isn't until you take action that you realize the ability, talent, and greatness you possess within.

When I was sixteen, I can remember watching motivational speakers, and wondering if I would ever have enough to say to fill an hour. Then came the time when I wondered if I would ever know enough to speak for four hours. Once I mastered four hours I wondered if I would ever have enough knowledge and experience to present a two-day seminar. I learned that once I acted on these goals, not only did I grow, but my fear began to dissipate. And with each action, more opportunities were made available to me. I realized that I didn't have to be great to start, but in order to be great I would have to start. Just like driving the car the first time. By doing what is wrong we often learn what is right. I had to stop expecting to be perfect and instead decide to start taking action. When I looked at my friends in school, I have on occasion asked myself, "What makes me different in terms of achievement?" The answer is without doubt—failure. Yes, failure. In my quest to achieve I am willing to fail, because I see failure as a necessary part of the road to success.

If, for example, you are unhappy with your parents, friends, or job, but do nothing about it, then nothing will change. Like I said before, good intentions don't cut it. People don't care about what you meant to do. They care about what you did. Your teacher doesn't care that you meant to turn in your homework assignment on time. She cares whether or not you did turn it in on time.

Unfortunately, many people fool themselves into believing that their ship will come in without taking any significant action. Nothing in life is simply handed to you. People forget that a plane is full throttle as it takes off and begins climbing the blue sky, and the pilot doesn't back off the throttle until the optimum momentum and altitude is reached.

One way to increase your ability to act is to stand up to the inner voice that causes you to live less than your true potential. If you decide that something is important to you, turn off that inner critic. I don't know if a dog has ever chased you before or not, but it's not exactly a pleasant experience. I can remember jogging on a few occasions when mean-looking dogs ran up attempting to chase me and even bite my leg. Instinctively, I would attempt to run away only for the dog to chase me more. Since then, however, I have learned to stop right where I am, turn around, stare directly into the dog's eyes, walk right toward it, and in a stern and unwavering voice tell it, "Get out of here!" Nine times out of ten, dogs will immediately turn around and run off. This is how you must be with your fears and your critics. Face them with confidence. Does this take courage? Yes! Will the thought pass through your mind, "What if it doesn't work?" Yes! Again, this is all a part of the process.

When taking action on your dreams, you have to momentarily disassociate from all that could go wrong and all the reasons why something won't work. You must change your focus from what could potentially go wrong to what could be gained by taking action. Then, in that fleeting moment of suspending fear, you must take action.

On the first success tape I ever listened to by Jim Rohn, he taught, "Always act when the emotion is high." Take action when the inspiration is present and strong. Don't allow the emotion to leave without first taking some sort of action. Take advantage of these opportunities when they arise. They come at odd times and few

"Always act when the emotion is high."
–Jim Rohn

in number. By taking action when the inspiration is strong, you begin to create momentum. Whether large or small, each action you take will give you continued motivation and a massive desire to keep going.

Sometimes you will be required to take action without clearly seeing the end result. Often the path is not clearly laid out in front of you. You cannot expect to know everything before you take action. You cannot expect to have the perfect strategy planned out before you decide to act. Action requires faith. Sometimes you just have to jump in. Now, don't get me wrong. Strategy is important, but if you spend all your time strategizing and never taking action, you'll remain where you are. There are times when even an effective strategy can't be formed without first taking action—even if it is a few simple steps. I like what the creator of the shows: *Survivor, The Apprentice,* and *The Contender*—Mark Burnett says, "Jump in–even if you don't know how to swim." Mark continues, "It's about taking action. Nothing will ever be perfect, and nothing can be totally planned. The best you can hope for is to be about half certain of your plan and...[be] willing to work hard enough to overcome the inevitable problems as they arrive."

It can also be beneficial to break big goals down into smaller ones. If the action you are about to take creates overwhelming fear, then scale down the amount of risk and gradually increase it. In *Success through a Positive Mental Attitude*, W. Clement Stone states,

> Roger Bannister reasoned that a man ran a single quarter-mile faster than he ran the four quarters of a full mile. So he trained himself to think of the four quarters in the mile separately. In his training he would dash a quarter mile, then jog a lap around the track to rest. Then he would dash another quarter mile. Each time he aimed to run the quarter in 58 seconds or less. Fifty-eight times four equals 232 seconds, or three minutes and 52 seconds. He ran to the point of collapse. Then he would rest ... When he finally ran his great race, it was in 3 minutes, 59.6 seconds!

> Finally, someone had broken the four-minute-mile

time barrier.

Doing a little at a time is an excellent strategy that can help your confidence grow. If you want to learn how to high jump, you wouldn't start out at six feet. Maybe start out at three feet and work your way up. In mathematics you don't start out multiplying 3,494 x 26,589. You start out with 2 + 2.

> You must be willing to put yourself on the line...

Although you take action, your goals will not always unfold as you planned. When you don't get the outcome that you anticipated, make sure you are using the most effective strategy. You may possess commitment, belief, or any other principle in the book, but if you're utilizing a weak strategy, I've got news for you—success is unlikely to happen. If you want to go south and your path is taking you west, it is improbable that you will get where you want to go.

In developing or changing your strategy, be sure to take into account your timing and circumstance. The same strategy won't always work in a different set of circumstances. You must be willing to change your approach when you discover you are not producing the desired outcome. Don't be so locked onto one approach that you become inflexible. If you know that the action you are taking is not giving you the results you want, then change your strategy or approach. In other words take constant action.

I like what George Bernard Shaw said: "People are

always blaming their circumstances for what they are. The people who get on in this world are the people who get up and look for the circumstances they want, and if they can't find them, make them."

Don't be fooled into believing that dreaming and hoping alone are enough to get you what you want. Sitting on the couch watching television or playing video games won't make it happen for you either. You must be willing to put yourself on the line—to defy the odds. Once a person puts himself on the line, he realizes he is much more capable than he previously thought. Once you know what you want, commit yourself to taking action. Action leads to further motivation and desire. This momentum leads to more action. Once you have this momentum, the process of achieving your goals becomes unbelievably exciting.

Today I make the commitment to take action on these goals: _____

_____

_____

_____.

CHAPTER 9

MAINTAINING A WINNING PERSPECTIVE

Law #8

IN THE REAL WORLD, MOMENTS OF devastation are likely to come your way. Discouragement may creep up at the slightest miscarriage of your deeds. There isn't one person on this planet who doesn't experience misfortune—we all do. It's part of the process. Consequently, setbacks drive some people to fight harder. For others, it provides a reason to quit. The difference is all in your perspective and response.

Although we are unable to control every situation in our lives, such as, a family member dying, a parent who has been laid off from work, the timing of your car breaking down, or being rejected to the college of your dreams. However, we can control how we respond to them and what meaning we assign to an outcome. Think about this the next time you have a bad hair day, your clothes don't fit right or have poor complexions. We all have good days and we all have bad days. There are days when we feel we are in a funk! Learning to master the art of interpretation and controlling your perceptions is a precious skill regardless of how difficult situations may be. Communicating effectively about these situations can make all the difference in your day–to–day experience.

A number of years ago I met with a well-known author and speaker who has influenced millions of people. He was battling a rare form of cancer and given only eighteen months to live. My idea was to capture his insight, wisdom, humor, outlook on life, and how he was coping with cancer. I asked if I could interview him and record it. I suggested that once it was produced and sold in stores I would pay him a royalty on the project. He agreed and asked me to meet him at his office in one week. Over the next week I began intently preparing my dialogue, and the questions I would ask. All week I memorized and imagined how the interview would successfully unfold.

The day we agreed upon had arrived and after setting up the recording equipment, we began our interview. It went very well and was even a little emotional as he shared glimpses of his personal battle with the horrible disease. He sincerely opened up to me and shared many of his deep and personal feelings, I was humbled. Then about an hour into the interview, I looked down and to my surprise, I noticed I hadn't pushed the record button. I was shocked and even devastated. Immediately, I felt the blood in my body rush to my face. Although, I was embarrassed, I maintained my composure. Finally, our interview ended and I told him I would get back with him in a few weeks. I was too embarrassed to tell him what had just happened.

Walking away from that experience I had a choice as to how I could communicate this experience to myself. I could have either said, "I'm a failure," "I can't do anything right," or I could simply interpret the situation as a learning experience—one I would never make again. I chose the latter interpretation. Not long after that experience I told him what had happened, and he too had a choice as to how he would respond to it. Fortunately he also chose to see it as a learning experience—I was off the hook.

As I travel the country and share this story, it inevitably causes audiences to gasp in disbelief. Many have even approached me after I share the experience and suggest that it possibly worked out just as it should have. They insist that the experience was meant for this person and myself alone. This too is a wonderful perspective.

In his book, *Psycho-Cybernetics*, Maxwell Maltz says it is vital to separate who you are from your performance. Here is why this is extremely important: as someone once stated, "If you are what you do, when you don't, you aren't." In other words, if your internal communications, performance, and self-worth are all based on your performance alone, what happens when you do not perform well? If all your self-worth and happiness is tied up in making the football team or making the beauty pageant, then what happens when you don't make the cut? Good and bad, your self-esteem and self-worth may resemble a roller coaster going up and down, rather then a constant and determined line.

> "You must seperate your-self from your performance."

Too many people allow their performance to dictate the way they feel about themselves. This is not always healthy. For example, if you give one speech that turns out unfavorably, that doesn't mean that you are a poor speaker. For whatever reason, it simply means that you didn't do well during that particular speech. The same is true if you set out after a goal only to find rejection and defeat. It doesn't necessarily mean that people are rejecting you personally. If you begin taking action on a goal and fall on your face in the process, that doesn't mean that your goal isn't possible. The truth is, most goals are not accomplished overnight. In fact, the average business or idea fails a dozen times before ever finding success. Even Michael Jordan, the legendary basketball player, was cut from his High School basketball team his sophomore year, but he didn't let that stop him.

If you make a mistake, that doesn't mean that you personally are a mistake. If you failed at something, it doesn't mean you are a failure. Often people allow a mistake or failure in one area to bleed into other areas of their lives. They take a small event and blow it out of all reasonable proportions. They beat themselves up over the mistake and take them personal. In some cases they pity themselves or become the victim of their misfortune. This is destructive!

The first time I ever gave a speech in public, I was a senior in high school. Mr. Sams, one of my all-time favorite teachers, approached me and encouraged me to enter a statewide speaking tournament. This meant that I would have to speak on a particular subject for five minutes in front of a panel of judges. Initially, I declined Mr. Sams' invitation, but he continued to encourage me. The one thing that I appreciated Mr. Sams for was that he believed in me. Finally I relented, and told him I would enter the tournament. Mr. Sams told me the subject to which I was to speak was "goals." I immediately began preparing my speech.

I practiced reciting my speech twenty or thirty times. The day I was to speak had arrived and I was prepared. I felt confident. My name was called and I entered the room filled with judges. They smiled as I walked to the front of the room. After wishing me luck, they invited me to start as soon as I was ready. I began, and I was on a roll. In the zone, the words rolled right off my lips. I could tell they were impressed. Upon finishing my speech, they told me I had done a great job. I left the room as another student entered. Mr. Sams asked how

I did, "I think we are going to win this." I replied. Toward the end of the day, right before they awarded the winners, the judges approached Mr. Sams and asked if they could visit with him. Initially, I knew not the reason, but when Mr. Sams emerged from the room I knew something wasn't right. He pulled me aside and told me that I had won first place, then there was a pause.

"But," he said, "They can't award it to you."

I asked, "Why?"

"I gave you the wrong subject to speak on," he replied.

"What?" I said.

He responded, "There has been a mistake. They gave me the wrong information. You were supposed to speak on The Free Enterprise System, not goals." He continued, "Technically we should be disqualified, but the judges were so impressed with you that they will be awarding you third place."

I had placed third in the tournament, however the way I communicated internally about the minor misfortune made all the difference. As you can see, I could have become upset toward Mr. Sams or myself. I could have let the embarrassment of speaking on the wrong subject determine that speaking was not for me. However, I chose none of these. Instead, Mr. Sams and I laughed about it. Over the years we've laughed numerous times about the experience. Deep down I knew that whatever the result, I had truly done my best and that it resulted in a great performance.

Achievers realize that there is no such thing as failure, because they seek to grow from each setback. Although not always a comfortable experience, achievers choose to see adversities as assets rather than liabilities. Most high achievers say they are thankful for their

"Every adversity has the seed of an equivalent or greater benefit."
—W. Clement Stone

setbacks because those experiences were viewed as a source of strength that helped prepare them for opportunities that would come next.

It is important to look for the blessings in disguise. W. Clement Stone said, "Every adversity has the seed of an equivalent or greater benefit." In these moments, you must say this to yourself and believe that something good will come of this. Then ask yourself, what is good about this problem? How can this problem benefit me? When you ask these questions, your brain will eventually find the answers. No matter how bleak, there is always a blessing in disguise. If you or your parents have been laid-off from work, you can decide to perceive it as though there is a better opportunity elsewhere. Maybe the universe was simply helping you or them with making a decision that you knew you needed to make but kept putting off. This job change is now providing you an opportunity to grow. If someone in a relationship left you, possibly it is time for you to move on and find someone who will treat you better, someone that is right for you. Think about it, have you ever been faced with something terrible that actually turned out to be a blessing? I'm sure you have. It all has to do with how you look at it. Even anxiety can be good if it leads you to do something productive. Dyslexia can even be good if you can find a productive use for it, and people have. An apparent weakness can actually be a strength if you make it so. Whatever you look for you will find.

There is a legend told of a young man who grew up in a poor village. When he was old enough he left the village in search of riches. The villagers were happy for him and patiently anticipated his return, because they put all their hopes for the future in him. Some years later he returned to the village. The villagers were excited to see what fortunes he had brought back. After they gathered around, he reached into his pocket and pulled out three little seeds. They scoffed and ridiculed him, complaining that his time away had been a waste. The people of the village were let down. All of the hopes and dreams they had placed in this young boy had quickly vanished. After enduring a barrage of scoffing and ridicule, the young man turned and walked to a nearby field and planted the seeds in the ground. The three seeds were cocoa seeds and as the legend goes, the main crop today in Ghana is cocoa plants because of this one young man. This man didn't see his three little seeds as failure; he saw them as the answer.

Life can be full of problems or it can be full of wonderful blessings. It is all a matter of how you look at it. Some people find difficulty in every opportunity and others find opportunity in every difficulty. Which way do you lean? Even in the worst of circumstances, history shows this power in action. In his classic book, *Man's Search for Meaning*, Viktor Frankl points out that many of those who survived the Nazi concentration camps said that they "benefited from the captivity, seeing it as a growth experience," although it was a horrendous time. Many came out of that experience having discovered God, and the realization that they could handle much more than they had previously thought. On the other hand, there were also those that saw their captivity differently and found ways to end their lives prematurely. The difference between the two was primarily the way they communicated internally about the experience—in other words, perspective. Whatever you focus on and the meaning you give it, will determine your experience. It's up to you. As a result of this power you possess, it would be unbelievably useful to stop blaming life and your circumstances for your unhappiness. You have choice. Use it!

> Some people find difficulty in every opportunity and others find opportunity.

In 1973, W. Mitchell was driving his motorbike when he was distracted and took his eyes off the road for a second too long. When he finally looked forward, he realized he was about to collide with a semi truck that had come to a stop in front of him. In that split second he made the decision to lay down the bike. After sliding more than one hundred feet and breaking many bones in his body, the gasoline cap popped off and spread fuel all over the ground. The motorbike caught fire, burning 65 percent of his body with third-degree burns. You would think this would be enough to experience in one lifetime, but after leaving the hospital six months later, he and three of his friends took off in an airplane. Once they reached ninety feet in the air, the plane lost power and dropped like a rock. There were four people on the plane that day and three walked away unscarred. The fourth person, W. Mitchell, was unable to move his body. His lower back was crushed, and he was paralyzed from the waist down. Unlike most people, he didn't give up or lose his zest for life. Instead he said, "Before, there were ten thousand things I could do. Now there are nine thousand. I can either dwell on the one thousand I've lost, or focus on the nine thousand things left." After these experiences, he has gone on to be a mayor, congressional nominee, gubernatorial candidate, and million–dollar businessman. Today he is also a motivational speaker. This greatness lies within each of us.

Often, it is through pain that we grow the most. There are libraries full of books about men and women who have turned tragedy into triumph. Many achievers started off with very little resources and managed to find enormous success. Similarly, there are many who were given every opportunity, all the love and encouragement, and still they turned out broke and depressed. It is never the events or circumstances themselves that determine whether you are successful or defeated. More importantly, it is how you perceive and respond to your challenges that make the difference.

Mastering the habit of interpreting each setback as an opportunity or blessing in disguise will give you the energy to push forward when the future looks dim. Just like no problem is permanent, each setback is not an attack on you personally. I remember there were times when in the face of setbacks all I could do was think to myself, "Well, at least one day this will make a good story." There are times when we must simply trust that the circumstances are for our own good.

Remember to capitalize on small wins. Find the small victories. Realize that you cannot run faster than you are able. But as long as you are making progress, sooner or later you will find the success you are looking for.

Even the discovery of "Post-It Notes" was born as the result of a failure. In the 1970s, chemist Spencer Silver was working for the 3M company to improve the acrylic adhesives used on their tapes. As a result of an accident, he created an adhesive that wasn't very sticky, yet wouldn't dry either. This failure gave birth to a new idea that is now used in homes and offices around the world.

It is all in how you look at it. When things don't turn out as you would like them to—as occurs from time to time—choose to see the momentary setback as an opportunity to change and grow. One of the greatest basketball coaches of all time, John Wooden once said, "Things turn out best for those that make the best of the way things turn out."

Today I make the choice to re-interpret and perceive my current circumstances or this specific past event in a more beneficial way: _____

_____
_____.

CHAPTER 10

CREATING YOUR OWN SUCCESS TEAM

Law #9

DALE CARNEGIE USED TO TEACH THAT there is no such thing as a self-made man. In the real world, no success is achieved by a single person. No one stands alone. In the end, none of us makes it to the top by ourselves.

For this reason, achievers understand the importance of creating a home-court advantage. In order to get what you want, it will be necessary to surround yourself with people who can help you get it. You must associate with people who compensate for your weaknesses. Partner with those who are smarter than you. Create associations and friendships that you can draw upon for ideas, energy, perspective, motivation, and accountability.

Whether you study great achievers in any field—athletes, actors, teachers, parents, leaders, managers, and so on, you will find that they all had the benefit of either being mentored and influenced by other people. These associations helped to catapult them forward.

Albert Einstein said, "Many times a day I realize how much my own outer and inner life is built upon the labors of my fellow men, both living and dead, and how earnestly I must exert myself in order to give in return as much as I have received."

Earlier I said that the same level of thinking that has brought you this far in your life is not enough to take you where you want to go. Making an effort to wisely and consciously choose your associations and the influences you surround yourself with can and will have a dramatic impact on your thinking, your beliefs, your habits, and your achievements. In other words, it has a dramatic effect on your life. In fact, if you want to see your future, look at your friends. Remember that you become the average of the five people you hang around.

> If you want to see your future just look at your friends.

Napoleon Hill spoke of the "Master Mind" principle, which he defined as "the coordination of knowledge and effort, in a spirit of harmony, between two or more people, for the attainment of a definite purpose." In his book, *Think and*

Grow Rich, Mr. Hill tells of Henry Ford, who became one of the wealthiest men in America in a short period of time.

> Mr. Ford's most rapid strides became noticeable from the time he became a personal friend of Thomas A. Edison... Go a step further and consider the fact that Mr. Ford's most outstanding achievements began from the time that he formed the acquaintances of Harvey Firestone, John Burroughs, and Luther Burbank ... Through his association with Edison, Burbank, Burroughs, and Firestone, Mr. Ford added to his own brainpower the sum and substance of the intelligence, experience, knowledge, and spiritual forces of these four men.

In *The Success Principles*, Jack Canfield co-author of the *Chicken Soup for the Soul* series told of how his partnership with Mark Victor Hansen began. While having breakfast one morning Mark asked Jack, "What are you up to? What are you excited about?"

Jack proceeded to tell him about the *Chicken Soup* idea. Immediately, Mark said, "I want to be your partner on this book. I want to help you write it."

Jack replied, "Mark, the book is already half written. Why would I let you be my partner at this stage of the project?"

"Well," he replied, "a lot of stories you tell, you learned from me. I have a lot more you haven't heard. I know I can get great stories from lots of other motivational speakers, and I can help you market the book to people and places you've probably never even thought of."

As they continued to talk, Jack realized that Mark would be a great asset to the project. So they struck a deal. After selling almost 100 million *Chicken Soup* books worldwide, Jack went on to say that as a result of that one conversation, it has been worth tens of millions in book royalties and licensing income to Mark and himself. The same can happen for you. Unforeseen power and opportunities will arise when you spend the majority of your time with the right people.

Our environment and those with whom we associate will have a profound impact on who we become and how much we achieve. The natural world also demonstrates this effect. For example, look at the ways in which certain species of fish grow according to their environment. Put them in a small aquarium and they remain small even into adulthood. Release them into a larger body of water and they grow to their full-intended size. Human achievement appears to function the same way.

Attitudes, demeanor, and energy are contagious. Like a sickness, if you want the flu, hang around people that have the flu. You've heard the phrase "Lie down with dogs and you come up with fleas." If you are not the kind of person who steals, hang around people who steal and watch what happens. As a result of your surrounding influences, you may just give in, and sooner or later you may be stealing too. People eventually wear down. Slowly, your beliefs and standards may change, and you begin rationalizing that it is okay to steal. You say, "I'm not going to drink. I'm not going to have sex or do drugs." or "I won't speak like that." Well, I've got news for you; if you continue to associate with people who engage in those behaviors it is just a matter of time before you engage in the same behavior.

Although your friendships may start out harmless they can begin shaping your life in many ways, both positively and negatively. Half way through my junior year a new student moved into our school. He was friendly, played sports, and was well liked. His name was Eric, and my friends and I quickly invited him to hang out with us. We were good—we didn't drink, smoke, and tried hard to stay out of trouble—other than wrapping a few houses in toilet paper, of course. Every morning we gave Eric a ride to school and we would hang out after school. But after a period of time Eric decided to hang out with a new group of friends. I was worried because this group had a reputation of getting into trouble. It wasn't long before we hardly saw Eric at all. Periodically, I would hear that Eric was attending parties around town. It was there that he started drinking, smoking, and living on the edge.

Then one day I noticed him walking the school hallway holding a pink slip in his hand. I greeted him and asked about the pink slip. With his head down he told me he was dropping out of school.

I asked him, "Why?"

Looking down, he said, "My girlfriend?"

"What about your girlfriend?" I responded.

"Well, she is pregnant and I need to provide for her and our baby," he said.

I put my arm around him and said, "Oh, Eric..." That was the last time I ever saw him. After graduating from high school I moved to Taiwan for two years. While in Taiwan I received a letter with a newspaper clipping. It read that while Eric was walking home after a dentist appointment he walked across the Blackjack Creek Bridge. Half way across the bridge, sizing up his life, he decided to jump. He had taken his own life. As I look back, I can't help but clearly see the subtle impact his new group of friends had on him. His peer group influenced his decisions early on, which soon created an avalanche of decisions that put him in a downward spiral.

Am I saying that if you hang out with the wrong people you could kill yourself too? Of course not, what I am saying is, his associations definitely had a role to play. Had Eric not changed his group of friends, there is a good chance he would still be alive today. The friends you hang with or the people you spend time with *will* make the difference in the quality of your life. I promise!

You may be the fastest runner in the world, but if you are running in mud, you'll be hindered and never set the record you are capable of achieving. Likewise, if you spend time with the wrong people, their influence, like mud, could prevent you from maximizing your true potential.

In general, there are two types of people and dominant attitudes they possess: those who are positive and those who are negative. To get the most out of yourself, it is vital that you spend your time with positive people.

Positive people are those who take charge of problems rather than complain about them. They don't criticize. They have the tendency to look for the good in people and their situation. They are solution-oriented. They make an effort to minimize problems rather than enlarge them. They keep their eye on the big picture, making the best out of each situation and even ask for learning opportunities. They seek to squeeze lemonade from the lemons of life!

Good things seem to happen to positive people. They seldom get depressed and rarely cause others to become discouraged or depressed. When you share your goals with them, they are naturally supportive. They are happy, which makes them pleasant to be around. They smile and cause others to do the same. They are leaders.

I suspect you have also been around people who were just the opposite; people who are negative, cynical, or even destructive. These people have been identified as "toxic" people. They lack faith and they criticize. They are backstabbers and bullies. They are the people who drain and drag you down. It is their mission to tell you how and why things can't be done. The more you strive to succeed the more they strive to prevent success from happening. It may not always be noticeable. They may be subtle, sitting back and even snickering. The moment you make a mistake, they are quick to point it out.

Although you are responsible for your emotions, these people can cause you to feel stressed, insecure, and even sick inside. If you spend much time with them, they can drive up your blood pressure and impact your health. When hard times come, they blame others rather than take responsibility. They complain when things don't go their way, quickly determining that their failures are someone else's fault. All of this leads them to the dangerous spiral effect of the victim mentality.

If you find yourself associating with these negative people, my advice is to turn, run, and never look back. Charles "Tremendous" Jones had a phrase that he often shared: "You will be the same person in five years that you are today except for the people you meet and the books you read." If you find yourself surrounded by people who are destructive, let them go. It is not worth the price.

Granted, I know you are probably thinking that you can't, because it's your brother or sister, parent, or good friend who is negative. If this is the case then you have three options to consider. The first is to be a leader and inspire them through your example. Dr. Phil says, "We teach people how to treat us by our own actions and behaviors." The second is to spend as little time as possible with this person. Third, keep your goals and dreams quietly hidden from them. W. Clement Stone said,

"Confide in no one but those that have genuine sympathy with your cause and an understanding of your possibilities. Otherwise, keep your plans to yourself and let your actions speak." If you're at a family dinner or have been invited to a party, then attend, but don't include them in your goals and dreams. You don't need their approval anyway!

I am not suggesting that you align yourself only with people who like you and blindly tell you what you want to hear. Yes, having these people in your life is important, but there is something more. It is important to associate with those who add to your reservoir; people who cause you to stretch to be better. If you want to become a great tennis player, you wouldn't play with someone who has less skill than you or even equal. You would play with someone slightly better than you.

Get around people who encourage and support you. J. Willard Marriott, founder of Marriott Hotels had a statement that he lived by: "Good timber does not grow with ease. The stronger the wind the stronger the trees." The great quarterback Steve Young once spoke on the concept of influence and his association with Joe Montana. He said that even though he was offered contracts to play on other teams as the starting quarterback, he rejected them because of the value he gained by playing under the great Joe Montana. He said that if he were going to be the best, he

> Get around people who encourage and support you.

had to associate with the best.

At seventeen, Steven Spielberg spent his days at Universal Studios watching directors and film crews. He followed them around asking questions, desiring to learn all that he possibly could—which eventually led the directors to ask for his input. He also studied the work of Martin Scorsese and Francis Ford Coppola. Eventually he found kinship with George Lucas, who said, "We were always willing to help each other make the best movie." Steven Spielberg spent the majority of his time with those who could not only help him grow, but also who could provide a different perspective, knowledge, experience, and intelligence.

Align yourself with those who are qualified. If you want to be a millionaire, it wouldn't be wise to take advice from someone who doesn't have a dollar in his bank account. Get around other millionaires. Learn from them. If you want to own your own business, associate with people who are successful at running their own businesses. If you want to be a great athlete—train with other great athletes. If you want a lot's of friends, learn how to be a good friend.

Surround yourself with people who have vast experience in your area of interest. You may even need to actively seek them out. In the beginning you may not know anyone who can provide this level of mentoring, or you may not yet have become the type of person who will attract such a mentor. Thus, your mentors and influences will be the books you read, the audio programs you listen to, and the seminars you attend. These resources make wonderful mentors, providing you with great ideas, motivation, confidence, knowledge, and greater belief in yourself and your possibilities. Anthony Robbins said, "No matter how grim your world is, if you can read about the accomplishments of others, you can create the beliefs that will allow you to succeed."

Geese are excellent examples of creating a success team. Have you ever noticed that geese fly in a V formation? Have you ever wondered why that is and what benefit it provides? Some time ago I came across research which concluded that as each goose flaps its wings it creates an "uplift" for the birds that follow. This strategy allows each bird to save 50 percent of its energy by reducing the drag. As a result geese can fly 71 percent farther as a group in this formation than one can fly alone. The same is true of people. If you want to see what your future will look like, look at the people with whom you spend most of your time. The people you consistently associate with will have a dramatic impact on where you end up in life.

Make the commitment today to develop yourself in such a way that you will begin to attract people into your life who will greatly contribute to the achievement of your goals.

Below is a list of those individuals I desire to associate with. The team I want to create that will contribute to the achievement of my most important goals includes: _____

_____

_____.

THE POWER OF FOCUS

Law #10

ONE MAJOR REASON PEOPLE NEVER GET what they want is because they lose focus on what is most important. Og Mandino said, "Too many of us never realize our greatness because we get sidetracked by secondary activity." We decide to go after a goal, and before you know it we start "majoring in minor things." We start dabbling a little over here and a little over there, and wind up never getting closer to achieving our goals. I'm always amazed at how many college students change their majors and even the college they attend, knowingly setting them back in time from obtaining their degrees. This is largely because they are not clear about what they want in the first place. You've probably heard it said, "A man with one watch always knows what time it is. A man with two watches is never quite sure."

Achievers make a conscious effort to stay focused on those things that can really make a difference in their goals and lives. This can be difficult at times. We live in a world that is consistently vying for our energy and attention. From the moment we get up, advertising bombards us through the television, the Internet, E-mails, and even the telephone.

We are motivated by the desire to experience pleasure and avoid pain. Because we all want to be happy, we sometimes spread ourselves thin by engaging in these pleasurable, yet unproductive activities. If we are not careful, we may unknowingly trade what we want for the moment, for what we really want long-term. Be wise when spending time and energy in relationships, sports, hobbies, work and other activities or commitments. Ask yourself, how will this benefit me in the future? If your choices are not in alignment with what you want long–term, change them.

Achievers know that if they are going to accomplish anything of value they will need to concentrate all their energies. Concentration and focus provide an enormous power. Sunlight, when focused through a magnifying glass, will set a leaf on fire. Although the same sun may have been shining down on the leaf all day, the effect was not as powerful until the sunlight was focused and concentrated. The same is true with your goals. When all of your resources are focused on a single purpose, only then do you have the combining power to get what you want.

A story is told of a baseball team that was at the bottom of the league. That year a new coach was hired. The first thing the coach did was ask the pitcher, "What is your best throw?" The pitcher said, "I've got a good fastball, curveball, and knuckleball." The coach responded, "No, what is your best throw?" The pitcher replied he had a great fastball. The coach immediately told him, "That's all I want you to work on this whole season—your fastball." This team went from the bottom of the league to the World Series.

Concentration and focus means that you walk a straight line until the goal is accomplished. Charles Dickens said, "I could have never done it without ... the determination to concentrate myself on one subject at a time."

Trying to be a jack–of–all–trades often leads to being a master of none. Wearing too many hats, if not properly managed, can eventually become a definite obstacle keeping you from achieving your goals. Think about it, a world champion tennis player doesn't get to that level by spending his time and focus playing miniature golf. Likewise, a world-class stockbroker doesn't get to the highest level of his profession by spending time socializing around the office water cooler.

> Trying to be a jack of all trades often leads to being a master of none.

In the beginning, there might be a time and a place to take on many roles. When I first started my business, I was manager, graphic designer, salesman, recording engineer, and presenter—which included traveling. There is a time and a place for everything. However, there came a time when the demands of all these roles took their toll and prevented the business from growing at my desired rate. Realizing this, I began delegating anything that wasn't absolutely necessary for me to do myself.

In 1895, after studying the distribution of wealth in Italy, Vilfredo Pareto, an Italian economist, concluded that eighty percent of Italy's wealth was controlled by twenty percent of the people, and that twenty percent of the wealth was controlled by the other eighty percent. In the 1920s and 1930s Dr. Joseph M. Juran studied and coined the concept as the 80/20 rule or the Pareto Principle.

> Twenty percent of any group produces eighty percent of the overall results.

Twenty percent of any group produces eighty percent of the overall results. This is true of you as well; twenty percent of all you do will usually have a greater impact than the other eighty percent combined. Be sure that your thoughts and actions are focused on the top twenty percent of all your activities. If you have ten activities in front of you that need your attention, concentrate on the top two that will provide the greatest payoff. This will account for eighty percent of your overall results.

After interviewing two million achievers over the last fifty years, Marcus Buckingham wrote in his popular book, *Now, Discover Your Strengths*, "People who were truly successful in their chosen profession, from teaching to telemarketing, acting to accounting—discovered that the secret to their success was in their ability to discover their strengths, and to organize their life so that those strengths could be applied."

When pursuing your goals, spend most of your time engaging in your areas of strength. Jack Canfield teaches, "Identify your core genius, then delegate completely to free up more time to focus on what you love to do." If you are great at starting projects but weak at completing them, align yourself with people that are strong on finishing tasks. Drawing upon your strengths will be a major step toward success.

At times, keeping your eye completely focused will require you to say "no" or "let go" of roles that may be standing in the way. It has been reported that the late J.C. Penney believed the "wisest decision he ever made was to 'let go' after realizing he couldn't do it by himself any longer." Ask yourself if what you are doing right now is directly helping you achieve your goals. If you realize your strategy or actions are taking you in the wrong direction, change them.

There may come a time when you will need to make sacrifices. If sports, after school plays, work, or hanging out socializing with friends are standing in your way, stop! Taking on too many activities and roles can steal the necessary time and energy needed to master your craft.

It is important that you avoid anything that dilutes your energies. I remind you that this book is designed for people who want to achieve BIG goals. One definite rule of achievement is, once you know what you want, get single-minded and stay single minded until you have achieved your desired outcome.

Today I will eliminate or reduce these activities from my life:

_____

_____

_____.

These are the activities I will replace them with: _____

_____

_____.

Today I will put the majority of my focus in this area: _____

_____

_____

_____.

CHAPTER 12

CREATING A SENSE OF URGENCY

Law #11

T HE TRUTH IS THAT YOU DON'T HAVE A thousand years to live. In life, you are not afforded the luxury of unlimited time or a watch that lets you know how many days, months, or years you have left. For this reason, begin living with a sense of urgency—a sense that now is the time to start living your dreams.

Many, if not most people are living their lives by the credo "I'll do it tomorrow, next month, or next year." "One of these days I'll do it." Well, I've got news for you—life doesn't get easier. They imagine it will be easier to take action in the future than it will be to take action today. Once that day arrives, they are still standing at first base. How many people do you know that have great ideas and abilities but continue to put off taking action? What about you? What ideas or goals do you have, that you continue putting off?

> What ideas or goals do you have, that you continue putting off?

Life truly is just a flicker. You are here one day and gone the next. There are no guarantees that tomorrow will arrive, and yet the average person watches 6.5 hours of television and countless hours playing the Xbox per day.

Some people wait around hoping that their knight in shining armor will arrive. They secretly hope their dream life will knock on the door. If you are waiting for someone to hand you your dreams, I've got news for you, it's not going to happen! Life is not that easy. And it is this attitude that causes so many to "go to their graves with their music still in them," as Oliver Wendell Holmes put it. Many people have great intentions and ideas, but those alone won't take you very far. You actually have to do something and, more importantly, you have to do it now.

Stop waiting for your circumstances to improve before you act. Stop waiting for the perfect moment to arise. When opportunities reveal themselves—as they will from time to time—you mustn't let them pass without acting.

While in my early twenties, I looked for ways to increase my credibility in the marketplace and value before I set out to live my dream, which was to provide ideas and tools that could improve the quality of people's lives. One day some entrepreneurs asked me to help them start a business. They informed me that they had an idea that had not been put to the test in a particular region of the United States. After taking a few days to think about it and calculate the risks involved, I decided it was the time to act. Desire and opportunity had collided. I left my job working for a senator in Washington, D.C. and went to Utah. Within a year the business took off successfully and became the first multi million-dollar company I helped build.

A few years later, the same group with whom I had started the business came to me with a new idea for a second business. I accepted that opportunity and within a short period of time it also became a multi million-dollar company. In each case it was important to act immediately. Had I waited, the opportunity would have passed by. Timing was critical. This became evident when I noticed that it didn't take long before other companies started duplicating our ideas. As a result of acting when we did, however, we were able to maintain an edge in the marketplace.

In his book *Paradigms*, Joel Barker points out that in 1968, Switzerland dominated the world in watchmaking. In fact, the Swiss held 65 percent of the market place and more than 80 percent of the profits. For over one hundred years they were known for their watchmaking excellence. Then, within a mere ten years, their market share plummeted to less than 10 percent, leading to layoffs of fifty thousand out of their sixty-five thousand employees within three years.

Today America and Japan dominate the world in watchmaking. Joel asks the question, "How did the switch happen? Why did the Swiss, who dominated so massively, lose it almost overnight?" Because their beliefs prevented them from acting urgently on their new discovery. They were so confident in their mechanical watches that when the quartz watch, which was totally electronic and one thousand times more accurate was presented, they didn't act on it.

The Swiss thought no one would want a watch without gears, bearings, or a main spring. They were so confident, they didn't even protect the idea. The Swiss openly displayed the idea to the world at the Annual Watch Conference and both Texas Instruments and Seiko took one look at it and the rest is history.

The same thing happened when Howard Schultz came up with his idea for the espresso bar café. He had recently returned from a business trip in Italy and was impressed with their rich flavored espresso's and the way they were served. He was also impressed by the intimate relationship between café employees and their customers. When he returned to the U.S., he brought this idea back with him, but the owners of the organization he was working for at the time, a wholesale coffee company, didn't see the merit in his discovery. Consequently, he left the organization and started his own business. Today, Starbucks Coffee is one of the most successful companies in the U.S., with over seven thousand stores and new stores opening every day. What is even more amazing to think of are the thousands of people who had also visited Italy and had been equally impressed, but didn't have the vision and sense of urgency to act on it.

Howard Schultz said,

> I realized what I had to do. This is my moment, I thought. If I don't seize the opportunity, if I don't step out of my comfort zone and risk it all, if I let too much time tick on, my moment will pass. I knew that if I didn't take advantage of this opportunity, I would replay it in my mind for my whole life, wondering: What if? Why didn't I? This was my shot. Even if it didn't work out, I still had to try it ... It's one thing to dream, but when the moment is right, you've got to be willing to leave what's familiar and go out to find your own sound. That's what I did in 1985. If I hadn't, Starbucks wouldn't be what it is today.

Urgency is often confused with what is really important. What most people feel urgent about is often not important at all. Beware! If you acted urgently on every whim or desire, you would spread yourself too thin. When I speak of living with a sense of urgency, I am speaking of acting urgently once you know what you want, after having developed an effective plan, and know your priorities. I am

I am not suggesting that you—fire—ready—aim.

not suggesting that you—fire—ready—aim. Although there may be times when it is important to do so.

For example, when it comes to deciding that you have greatness within, you should act urgently. Not much planning is necessary for that one. Deciding that you are going to live with purpose would be another decision that you could act on urgently. Once you are clear about what you want and have determined your highest priorities in relationship to your goal, take action NOW! Don't put it off another day.

When it comes to time, high achievers don't complain about the long hours; they complain that the hours aren't long enough. They are striving to fill their time completely and effectively. In a *Fortune* magazine article, several of the most successful and highly paid executives in America were interviewed about their beliefs in relationship to time. The average yearly income among those interviewed was $1,380,000, and each had worked his way up from entry-level positions. When asked about time, they all saw time as a scarce resource and thus used their time very carefully. Benjamin Franklin said, "Do you love life? Then do not squander time, for that's the stuff life is made of."

This doesn't mean you have to become a work-aholic. Achievers realize that there are other important things in life, and they give attention to them. However, when it comes to achieving their goals, they recognize they don't have an unlimited supply of time. They simply choose not to waste time on meaningless activities.

After his embezzling conviction, William Sydney Porter didn't just sit in his prison cell twiddling his thumbs. He decided to write short stories and did so under the name of O. Henry. By the time he walked out of prison, he was one of the most popular short-story writers in the country.

If you have ideas, goals, and dreams within you, start living with a sense of urgency. Convince yourself that you have the ability. Convince yourself you are not too young. Remember that age is not a prerequisite for success. Some of the youngest people became the highest achievers. Whether it is Milton Hershey, the founder of the Hershey chocolate company, or the Parker Brothers who founded the game board company. Even Chef Bor R Dee began his cooking at twelve years old. There are examples of thousands of others, all at different stages in their lives, both young and old, who began living with urgency. This urgency not only enabled them to achieve their goals, but it also allowed them to make a contribution to their family, community, country, and even the world.

Imagine where you will be five years from now – ten years from now and start today. Today—this moment—is the only time you are guaranteed. There is no guarantee tomorrow will come. There is no guarantee the same opportunities that reveal themselves

> Remember that age is not a prerequisite for success.

today will be around tomorrow. Start living as though today were your last—not your first. The Pulitzer Prize–winning composer Gian Carlo Menotti said, "Hell begins on that day when God grants us a clear vision of all that we might have achieved, of all the gifts we wasted, of all that we might have done that we did not do." Stop living your life like you have a thousand years to live. Stop procrastinating, and start acting!

Today I will begin going after these two goals with a greater sense of urgency:

1._____.

2._____.

What are the benefits for acting on these two goals with more urgency? _____

_____

_____.

CHAPTER 13

NEVER GIVE UP

Law #12

QUITTING IS EASY. When things get difficult, most people simply give up. They don't have the vision or discipline to keep going when the going gets tough. History books are filled with countless stories of both men and women who knew the importance of perseverance and of the warnings of those who gave up! In fact, many described their failures and defeats as necessary stepping-stones toward their success.

Did you know that Walt Disney was turned down 302 times before the banks lent him the money to build Disneyland? Walt had a vision and stayed committed to fulfilling it. He realized that although he would encounter rejection, if he didn't give up on his vision, it wouldn't give up on him. Had this not been the case, millions of people each year wouldn't have the good fortune of experiencing "The Happiest Place on Earth."

Before Howard Schultz founded Starbucks Coffee Company, he spoke to 242 investors and all but 17 turned him down. Most of the 242 prospective investors told Howard that it was a crazy idea. But that didn't stop him.

Colonel Sanders was in his sixties when he decided his social security check wasn't enough to live on and went out to market his great idea. What was it? A chicken recipe that he thought everyone would want. He went from restaurant to restaurant asking if they would use his chicken recipe, and they thought he was crazy. The owners of the restaurants told him time and time again that they already had a chicken recipe, and they didn't need his. Finally, after hundreds of rejections somebody said Yes, and Colonel Sander's *Kentucky Fried Chicken* was born.

Thomas Edison was known to have encountered over 9,999 failures during the process of inventing the light bulb. He said, "Genius is one percent inspiration and ninety-nine percent perspiration!"

In the beginning, Dr. Seuss was rejected by twenty-eight publishers. The publishers considered the books "too outlandish to appeal to children." Abraham Lincoln spent most of his life failing before he became president of the

United States. In its first 28 attempts to send a rocket into space, NASA failed 20 times. Would you have kept trying after hundreds of failures? Unfortunately, most people wouldn't. Most people would have given up long before 302, 242, 28 or even a dozen failures. In

> Would you have kept trying after hundreds of failures?

fact, most people give up after one or two setbacks. Don't let this be said of you.

There is one guaranteed way you won't fulfill your dreams, and that is to simply quit on them. Unfortunately, most people do. The classic film, *Chariots of Fire*, depicts athletes competing against one another. One of the athletes, Harold Abrahams, while competing for a position on the British team, lost several heats against a Scottish runner. Abrahams complained to his girlfriend, "If I can't win—I won't run!" His girlfriend responded sharply, "If you don't run, you can't win."

Most people throw in the towel too soon. Had they given one more last effort and a little more time, they may have seen the harvest of their labors. We live in a culture of immediate gratification. It's a disease that causes us to think, if I can't have it now, it either isn't worth it or it must not be possible.

Like most teens, I too had dreams of making something out of my life. I often dreamed of owning my own business. One day I just decided to do it. I was sixteen and I wanted to prove to myself that it could be done. I thought, "why wait until I'm an adult, when I could get a head start now?" Thinking of all the different possibilities I decided to start a window cleaning business in my small town. This meant that I would need to come up with capital to by my equipment. So I spent the next few months working part time jobs. Once I had enough money my mother took me to a janitorial supply company to buy the equipment. I also realized I needed a business license, which cost me $20. The next step was to practice cleaning windows, so I started with my parent's house. My parents really loved that! Then it was time to start building a client base and I can still remember the first time I walked into the grocery store and asked for the manager. I was nervous, and when I met the manager I asked if I could clean his windows. He said he already had someone cleaning the windows and was not interested. At which point I thanked him for his time, and turned to leave. Just as I was about to leave his presence, he stood up and very boldly told me to "never do that again."

Confused, I turned around and said, "What?"

He said, "When I told you no and you simply accepted it." He continued, "If you are going to make it you have got to be persistent. In order to be successful you will need to sell yourself and your services. When someone rejects you, you must give him or her all the reasons why you are better than the next guy. You must understand that there are going to be people who will reject you and others who won't, but to increase your chances you have got to be confident in your services..."

That first experience taught me a lot. At first I was embarrassed, but deep down I knew he was trying to help me. I didn't get the store as a client, but it did teach me enough of a lesson that I went out and found thirty clients over the next few months. Did I encounter rejections in the process of gaining these clients? Of course! Probably thirty percent had initially rejected me. But I wasn't about to give up. I EXPECTED success.

One major cause of failure is the expectation of failure. Expectations control your life, so be clear about your expectations. Muhammad Ali didn't become great because he affirmed victory by stating, "*If* I win the fight," rather, he spoke in terms of "*When* I win the fight." Don't ever lose your spirit of determination. It will take you many places and provide more opportunities than you know.

> One major cause of failure is the expectation of failure.

Also, expect to be a winner, but don't expect to start out being one. Before you can become great at anything, it is likely that you will first be awful. Developing a skill or achieving a goal will be difficult at first. Furthermore, your goals don't always unfold exactly how you imagine they would.

Although many of the success stories you are familiar with may seem to have been instant successes, you don't always see the years of preparation and the many setbacks that contributed to their success. No matter the goal, results are produced much like compounding interest. You won't see any significant growth day to day, but unforeseen progress is being made.

If you believe in your goals strongly enough, and if you are committed to them, they will eventually bear fruit. Anything that is given consistent attention and energy, will grow. Success will eventually flow toward you and you toward success.

The unfortunate thing about giving up is that after you give up once, it becomes easier to do it a second time. This can

"Once you learn to quit, it becomes a habit."
–Vince Lombardi

lead to a third time and before you know it, you have made it a habit. Vince Lombardi, speaking in the locker room to one of his players said, "If you quit now, during these workouts, you'll quit in the middle of the season in a game. Once you learn to quit, it becomes a habit. We don't want anyone who will quit. We want 100 percent out of each individual, and if you don't want to give it, get out. Just get up and get out right now." You don't want it to be said of you that you were a quitter. You don't want to look in the mirror and think, "If I had just held on and pushed myself a little longer and a little harder I could have made it." Beware, quitting can become a way of life.

Someone said, "Stopping at third base adds no more to the score than striking out." If you have made a habit of giving up in the past, it is not too late to change. You can start by setting small goals for yourself and following through. As each goal is reached, you become satisfied, and it will motivate you to set another goal and eventually you will begin forming the new habit of following through and persevering.

The truth is, you can't get away from failure and rejection if you want to make something of yourself. This is life, and it happens to all of us from time to time. This is why learning to master your internal communication is extremely vital. You can't always control the events that take place in your life, but you can control what you do about them. Here are a few thoughts that can help.

In my seminars I teach that failure is only the end if you let it be. Keep in mind, failure is simply life's way of telling you to change your approach—to try something new. Sometimes nature has to step in to help because we don't always know what's best for ourselves. Pay attention to the feedback you are receiving. Just as Darwin taught, "only the fittest survive." In this case, the "fittest" are those who don't quit, but change their approach according to the feedback and continue moving forward. If you stay true to the vision, always looking for a way, a better strategy, continually in pursuit of what you want, you will eventually come though. Alexander Graham Bell said, "What this power is I cannot say. All that I know is that it exists, and it becomes available only when a man or woman is in that state of mind in which he or she knows exactly what he or she wants and is fully determined not to quit—until they find it." Failure is only the end when you decide to throw in the towel and give up. Otherwise, use failures as learning opportunities, bringing you closer to your desired outcome.

Even while I was writing this book, there were days I felt stuck and the ideas wouldn't come. There were days when I had no motivation to write. Each time I would take a moment, sometimes listening to music to help me get into the zone, and I would imagine the benefits of having a finished book. Most days this would help. Other days I simply had to discipline myself to begin writing, and eventually the desire and ideas would come. I also found that there were times when I would imagine my long-term disappointment if I didn't follow through. That seemed to help. If done carefully and periodically this too can provide the necessary drive.

Once you have the momentum—keep it going. You don't have time to relax. My friend and bestselling author, Bob Moawad says, "You don't want to coast unless you intend to go downhill." It may mean maintaining your momentum for thirty days, six months, a year, or even ten years, depending on your goal. Each act followed through carries with it the feedback that is necessary for further motivation.

> "You don't want to coast unless you intend to go downhill."
> —Bob Moawad

Sometimes you won't be able to see what lies ahead.

Sometimes you'll question yourself. Sometimes you'll look into the tunnel, and you won't be able to tell whether you see the light at the other end of the tunnel or a train coming right toward you. Sometimes you get confused and maybe a little discouraged because you can't see a solution. This is all part of the process.

No matter how difficult it may get, or how discouraging it may seem, just hang on because success is right around the corner. It is much like what Chuck Yeager experienced firsthand. He was the first person to break the sound barrier. When he was forty thousand feet in the sky and approaching the sound barrier, the rocket-powered X-1 fighter plane began to vibrate as though it was about to fall apart in midair. Although the thought passed through the minds of the controllers on the ground to abort the mission, it was simply not an option. Then, just as he and others thought the plane was about to fall apart, Yeager broke through the sound barrier and immediately thereafter, the ride became smooth. The noises and vibrations ceased. Sometimes you will think you are breaking down and can't handle it anymore. Maybe what is really happening is that you are about to break through.

Michael Jordan once said, "I've missed more than 9,000 shots in my career. I've lost almost 300 games. On 26 occasions, I have been entrusted to take the game winning shot ... and missed. I have failed over and over and over again in my life and that's why ... I succeed."

If you really want something important, it will often take great persistence. If you fall down, get back up and try again. Only those who persevere win the prize.

Today I will reaffirm to myself that I will endure and persist until this goal is achieved: _____

_____

_____.

CHAPTER 14

LIVE WITH PURPOSE

Law #13

IMAGINE PEOPLE YOU KNOW WHO ARE LIVING life without any overriding purpose and direction– particularly the adults around you. Whatever the image is, I'm sure it is not very attractive. They may not be the greatest examples of what you want your future to be like.

You see, without a vision for your life it is easy to get side tracked. Without purpose you would wander aimlessly through life. Many start out dreaming of multiple goals they want to accomplish someday. Yet, slowly they give up on their goals, making them a low priority.

Without purpose and desire every principle in

this book is virtually worthless. Yes worthless. Achievers understand the importance of living with a purpose. They know why they are here and they structure their life around that purpose. It gives them strength and causes them to look forward to each new day. Achievers have a magnetic sense and energy about themselves. They have an aura that people are attracted to. They are not merely trying to get *through* life; they are striving to get the most from life. They see each passing experience as an opportunity to grow. They strive to become the most they can possibly be.

> They are not merely trying to get <u>through</u> life; they are striving to get the most from life.

Achievers have a *can-do* spirit about them. They have the habit of finding reasons why things can work rather than why they can't. George Bernard Shaw said, "You see things and ask, why? But I dream of things that never were and ask, why not?" It is a beautiful thing when the spark is ignited and a vision is born.

People with purpose have hope for their futures. George Burns was a great example of this. In fact, his hundredth birthday party was sold out years before he turned one hundred! He expected to be in attendance. When President John F. Kennedy said, "In this decade we will put men on the moon," immediately the engineers and scientists started showing up for work earlier than normal and staying later. A new purpose and vision had changed the culture of their organization.

Many people lose their passion for life. If you believe this could happen to you, then wake up and question your direction and decide that you deserve more. That's exactly what happened to John and Peter Kockelman, who became the "incredible bungee brothers." Bungee jumping is the sport where you jump off a bridge attached to a cord and free-fall until you are snatched from death at the last second before hitting the ground. Before the Kockelman brothers were bungee jumpers, they were average Americans. Peter, the older brother, was an engineer, and John was a computer consultant. They had always wanted to start a business together. According to *Outside Magazine*, John saw his first bungee jump on a show called *That's Incredible*. John called his brother and suggested that they jump off a 140-foot bridge at the Don Pedro reservoir near Yosemite Park. Peter agreed and afterward called it "the most intense thrill I had ever experienced in my life. I felt like a spider dropping into the Grand Canyon on a thread." One year later, the younger brother, John, quit his job and decided to start a bungee-jumping business. He called Peter and urged, "Come on ... that is not what you are on this earth for, to sit there and be calm and sit and die slowly." Peter, the cautious one, was apprehensive but said, "The saddest thing I ever saw was the engineers who I worked with who had stayed thirty years beyond the time that they should have gone out and pursued a dream. So I decided to go for it." They chose to live their dreams and *Bungee Adventures* was born.

Howard Schultz, of Starbucks Coffee Company, embodied this inner need and purpose when he ventured out on his own and created one of America's most successful companies. He said, "I saw the move as consistent with my life's dream, my earliest desires to do something for myself and for my family, to achieve something unique, to be in control of my own destiny."

What is your destiny? What is your purpose? What is it that you want? What are your greatest interests? Maybe it's singing or someday writing a book. Maybe it's dancing, acting, or starting your own business. Perhaps you want to be a homemaker and be home to raise your children. What are you enthusiastic about? When asked the secret to his success, Mark Twain replied, "I was born excited." Thomas Edison said, "When a man dies, if he can pass enthusiasm along to his children, he has left them an estate of incalculable value." Ralph Waldo Emerson also observed, "Every great and commanding moment in the annals of the world is the triumph of somebody's enthusiasm."

What is your destiny? What is your purpose?

I feel sorry for so many who have given up and lost their zeal for life. Apathy annoys me! I once heard a line in a movie that has always stuck with me. A boy talking to his friend in the back of the school bus said, "If you sit in the back of the bus too long, you'll think you belong there."

Decide that you are going to live life to the fullest.

There are people all around us who die at thirty-five, yet are buried at seventy-five. It has been said that age has more to do with your psychology than it has to do with your chronology. Some of the oldest people I know are vibrant, healthy, and passionate. Yet, some of the youngest people I know are drained of energy—barely making it out of bed. I don't know what side of the fence you are on, but I hope you have determined that something in your life is worth going after.

I believe that living without purpose can be a major cause of unhappiness and even depression. People show up for work and occupy themselves by fixing their eyes on the clock. "One more hour until lunch, fifteen minutes until break and three more hours until I go home!" They do just enough to prevent themselves from being fired. Most people spend their whole lives living this way. The only thing they look forward to is their paycheck at the end of the week and the weekend that follows. I suppose you can't change everybody. Some people are content with being average. But *you* are not average. You wouldn't be reading this book if you were.

On the very real far side of living without purpose or striving to live a stress free life, is death. Research indicates that the average person who retires at age sixty-five dies within three years of retirement. Why? In addition to having no real sense of purpose, people are not continually growing, learning, or stretching, which I believe plays a significant role in keeping the brain alive and the body vibrant.

Acting on your purpose is the key that leads to happiness, fulfillment and satisfaction. Have you ever noticed that the word satisfaction ends with the word *a-c-t-i-o-n*? In Latin, the word satis means "enough." The ancient Romans knew that enough action would produce satisfaction.

Earlier I mentioned that without purpose none of the principles in this book would be applied effectively. If you don't have purpose, why would you push yourself so hard? Why would you even consider raising your standards? Why would you expect anything more than what you've accomplished in the past? You certainly wouldn't take the time to work on yourself and master your thoughts. Without purpose, life is slow and boring.

On the other hand, in order to get and keep the spark you must never lose your ability to think BIG, to think possibilities! I like what Andrew Carnegie, who became the richest man in the early 1900s once said, "If you want to be happy, set a goal that commands your thoughts, liberates your energy, and inspires your hopes." In the end, your purpose and big visions will be the fuel that will enable you to endure the hard times without giving up.

Mike Vance tells a story about the day Walt Disney died. While Walt lay on the hospital bed, outside the room were a number of reporters who were trying to get what would be Walt's last interview. Security was tight, and for obvious reasons, the reporters were not allowed in. But somehow one reporter was persistent enough and eventually got into the room. Walt gestured for him to lie down next to him on the bed. His energy was very low, and he could barely speak beyond a whisper. As the reporter lay there, Walt began pointing to the ceiling in an effort to describe in detail what Epcot and Walt Disney World would look like, an amusement park that wasn't scheduled to be built for another six years. Even while on his deathbed, he was focused on his purpose and was sharing his dream.

At birth we were all given special and individual gifts, talents, and capabilities. We were entrusted with these gifts and encouraged to nurture them. Stephen Covey in *The 8th Habit* wonderfully states,

> At birth we were all given special and individual gifts, talents, and capabilities.

> Latent and undeveloped, the seeds of greatness were planted. We were given magnificent birth gifts, talents, capacities, privileges, intelligences, opportunities that would remain largely unopened except through our own decision and effort. Because of these gifts, the potential within an individual is tremendous, even infinite. We really have no idea what a person is capable of ... The more we use and magnify our present talents, the more talents we are given and the greater our capacity becomes.

Begin living with purpose today and applying the

principles described in this book. You deserve it. No, I didn't say you are entitled to it, but you will deserve it if you pay the price. And not only will it benefit you, it benefits those around you, too. I love what Nelson Mandela said when he quoted Marianne Williamson in his inaugural speech as president of South Africa,

> We ask ourselves, who am I to be brilliant, gorgeous, talented, and fabulous? Actually, who are you not to be? You are a child of God. Your playing small doesn't serve the world. There is nothing enlightened about shrinking so that other people won't feel insecure around you. We were born to make manifest the glory of God that is within us. It's not just in some of us; it's in everyone. As we let our own light shine, we unconsciously give others permission to do the same.

This is greatness.

Living with purpose doesn't mean you have to conquer the world. Yet, it doesn't mean that you play small either. It only means you live life to the fullest, striving to be the best that you can possibly be. Novelist Robert Louis Stevenson wrote, "To be what we are, and to become what we are capable of becoming, is the only end in life."

All the inspirational books and audio programs in the world won't do anything for you if you are not first passionate, committed, and persistent. Go forward with a purpose, and unleash your individual greatness.

Jim Rohn called it *The Challenge.* "Let others lead small lives, but not you. Let others argue over small things, but not you. Let others cry over small hurts, but not you. Let others leave their future in someone else's hands, but not you."

No, not you. You are different. You are special. And you are unstoppable!

When I imagine living life with purpose, what do I see? _____

_____

_____.

What inner gifts and talents will I begin developing?

_____

_____

_____.

CONCLUSION

C ONGRATULATIONS! You have finished reading *If You Think You Can! for Teens*. It contains thirteen of the most important laws of not only achievement, but also life. Hopefully, you either discovered for the first time, or been reminded of, proven tools that will help you to tap the greatness you possess within. No matter how bleak or dim your circumstances or past may be, achievement is still possible for you. Your future has a lot to offer—if you will claim it and you can!

Here is one last suggestion: READ IT AGAIN. Yes!

Read the entire book or at the very least, review your notes and markings. Become familiar with each principle until they are all seared into your mind, both your conscious and subconscious minds. Read it once a month over the next year and I promise you, that what you have achieved today will be insignificant compared to what you'll have achieved twelve months from now.

These laws and principles work. They have worked for thousands of years and they are available to everyone who is willing to apply them.

Throughout the process of writing this book, I applied the thirteen laws. Today you hold it in your hands. This is evidence once again that application of the thirteen laws results in achievement. I specifically knew what I wanted. I imagined in advance, successfully receiving endorsements by these very high achievers. Once I made a definite commitment to complete this book, I immediately took action. I then, confidently asked for endorsements, and I persevered until the goal materialized.

As you read the book over and over, it will begin impacting your thoughts and beliefs, thereby positively impacting your performance. As a result, both large and small goals will materialize into reality. You will be amazed by the power of these simple truths as you read and apply them. Starting today, these principles will determine your future, whether you apply them or not.

I leave you now, but I pass on to you the same advice once given to me, "May the best of your past, be the worst of your future." Make your future the best that it can possibly be, because it is possible! You are in charge of your future. Dreams do come true!

The end—
is really the
beginning!

About the Author

TJ HOISINGTON is a bestselling author, speaker, business consultant, husband, and father. He is dedicated to helping individuals and organizations reach their potential by *unleashing their greatness within.*

TJ is the author of the international bestselling book, *"If You Think, You Can! Thirteen Laws that Govern the Performance of High Achievers"*, sold in 34 countries. He is the co-author of *"The Secret of the Slight Edge."* TJ is also the author of the historical fiction, *"Return to Robinson Island,"* which is the first *Swiss Family Robinson sequel* in over one hundred years.

TJ began his efforts at age sixteen when he discovered his life's purpose was to help people take control of their lives. Using the concepts he teaches, he formed his first company at sixteen and sold it two years later. Later, he was instrumental in starting two companies that both quickly became multi million-dollar corporations.

TJ has also advised, addressed, or consulted with corporations such as, *Seattle's Best Coffee, Century21, NBC, Toyota, Prudential, Ramada Inn, LegalShield, National Guard, Alaska Marine Lines, Bonita Bay Club*, and many more, including schools and non-profit organizations.

TJ Hoisington currently resides in Washington State with his wife and four children.

Acknowledgements

A special thanks to the following individuals who have in their own ways contributed to this book. I sincerely thank each of them for their time and insight that helped make this book a reality.

Thank you, Bob Moawad for your wisdom and understanding of the principles shared in this book. You were an amazing help. I am very thankful to Dick Anderson for the kind support he has given me over the years—starting at age sixteen. A special thanks to a good friend—John Richter. I met John while working with Anthony Robbins and his insights have been brilliant. Thank you Randy Vawdrey for being a wonderful visionary and conceptual thinker. Thank you, Tom Meagher for you amazing abilities for detail and understanding of grammar, punctuation, spelling, and flow of content. I wouldn't dare forget Hilary Turner, Linda Avery, and Betty Child—I appreciate your editing skills. Thank you Mary Ann Jackson for your understanding and critical eye—it was just what I needed. I thank my brother Steve Hoisington, who reviewed the manuscript and gave suggestions that enhanced the quality of this book. I am equally thankful for the many speacial teenagers who gave of their time, energy and wisdom. Thank you. Lastly, a special thanks to all those who kindly endorsed this book. I have definitely been blessed.

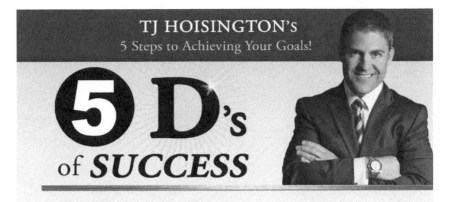

5 D's of *SUCCESS*

DESIRE Desire is the fuel for achievement. Going from where you are to where you want to be starts with a burning desire. Focusing this burning desire toward your goals and a better future creates boundless energy and reduces perceived limitations.

DEFINE You must know exactly what you want. Clarity is power. Take time to discover what you want to achieve, and make sure it's in alignment with your core values. Be specific. Be laser focused.

DECIDE The greatest power you have is CHOICE. Make a *TRUE decision* to achieve your goals. No excuses. No turning back. 100% COMMITMENT.

DWELL Impress the mind with images and thoughts of achieving your goals. Imagine yourself achieving the goal in the present tense – right now. Research consistently indicates that the subconscious mind cannot tell the difference between something that is vividly imagined with emotion and something that really happened. Dwelling 'daily' on your goals in detail will create strong beliefs, and once formed, your mind will work day and night helping you find the opportunities and resources that will make your goals a reality.

DRIVE Action is the winners' edge. Action is what separates high achievers from the low achievers and even the no-achievers. Once action is taken, you must maintain momentum. You do this by taking consistent action every day, regardless of its size. *Start today!*

<u>Notes:</u>

<u>Notes:</u>

"It's Possible!"

AYLESBURY
PUBLISHING